THE SECRET CODE OF SELF HEALING

BEGGINING - DEEPENING - LIBERATION

By Silvia Pla

catsanasen

The Direct Path to Your Tranformation

Silvia Pla Catania
The Secret Code of Self-Healing
Beginning - Deepening - Liberation
CATSANASEN
The direct Path

1nd Edition - Barcelona - Spain
136p. 21x14,8cm

ISBN: 978-84-09-22821-8
Depósito Legal: B 3078-2021

EDITED AND PRINTED BY SILVIA PLA

Design: María Verónica Racca

CONTENTS

Introduction 01
Catsanasen Method Self-Healing Guide 04
How to activate and regain the connection with intuition.. 04
Catsanasen Stages: Beginning, Deepening, Liberation . 06

BEGGINING 08
The flower of life 09
Guide to entry into a neutral and meditative state with the mind 12
Activating the right hemisphere and reconnecting it with the left one 14
Sacred Geometry 16
Dualities with Platonic solids 18
Subtle bodies 19
How to detect blockage in subtle bodies 22
Body with sphere 24
List of stages with their corresponding sphere 26
Subtle bodies and *chakras* 28
Application of geometry on *chakras* 30
Application of the energy spiral 31
Guide for applying geometry to the various subtle bodies 33
Tetrahedral star or *merkaba* 34
Tetrahedral star for men and women 36
The *merkaba* and the Christic energy network 38

DEEPENING 40
Geometry, elements and organs that are related 41
Archimedean solids 42
Chakras, subtle bodies and dimensions 43
Application of Archimedean and Platonic solids 44
Energy system, *chakras* and subtle bodies 45

Nadis, energy body 47
Acupuncture Meridians 49
Meridian Conception Vessel and Governor Vessel Meridian 53
Lymphatic system and circulatory system 55
Bone and muscle system 57
Types of tissue 59
Application of geometry for body aesthetics 61
Brain and spine 62
Corpus callosum and cranial nerves 63
Brain hemisphere functions 64
Brain and neurons 65
Brain hemispheres and geometry 67
Parasympathetic and sympathetic nervous system 69
Endocrine system glands 70
The sphenoid bone 72
Falx Cerebri 74
Spinal column 75
Geometry Application Guide 77
Cells, their components and DNA 79

LIBERATION 82
A comparison: geometry and cell division 83
Stages of the flower of life 85
Anatomical proportion 87
Bodies and its dimensions 89
Nadis, your energy body 91
Macro-energy connection with micro-energy 93
Energy healing chart 95
Main healing tetrahedron of the catsanasen method valid for every circumstance 97
Application of geometry for specific points 99
The connection with vibrations, colours and shapes 102
Connection with the higher self *chakras* 105
Colour application on subtle bodies 107
Ether connection 109

Connection to the fifth chamber of the heart 111
Pineal, pituitary and heart connection 113
Earth, body and planets connection 116
The *Merkaba* Star 118
Creating realities 119
The flower of life 121

INTRODUCTION

Atoms form molecules and molecules form bones, tissues, cells and everything in your body. And do you know what an atom is? It is energy.

All the dense and hard matter around you that you see is composed of molecules, and these molecules are in turn composed of atoms, and these atoms, in turn, are composed of energy, and this energy, you know who it obeys? it obeys you, your thoughts, your emotions and the force and intention you give them when you speak or think them.

Remember that you are the creator of your life and your thoughts are your magic wand, for this reason you need a clean mind, free of fears, limiting beliefs, negative and limiting thoughts because you are what you think.

We are beings capable of channelling energy without knowing that we actually are and without having any idea of what kind, how much and how, but we are constantly doing it and it is on the basis of this energy that we are alive.

We can condense it or use it, transmute it or transmit it, use it for our benefit or harm, we just have to discover the frequency in which we vibrate and heal, acquiring the vibration that will allow us to live in tune with the fullness, magic and harmony of the universal energy.

Thoughts, emotions and beliefs are the vehicles of this energy. These thoughts, beliefs or emotions can be personal, collective, cultural, family, ancestral, religious or institutional; they can be from this era or another, from this galaxy or others, they may be created an instant ago or a million years ago. Everything, absolutely everything, will influence us and make us vibrate.

All beings are connected to a huge and multidimensional individual, collective and universal energy network and we are literally always «On Line". Only the focus we consciously give to this energy or vibration will determine the materialization of the experience/reality we will live.

In our genetic pattern, in the unconscious, in the cells and

in the cellular sub-structures, are stored the memories that generate and project the situations and experiences that we are going to live, and this is where the Catsanasen influences energetically by modifying patterns, beliefs, thoughts, emotions and the information in your DNA. It could be said that human beings are like a group of thoughts that condensed into physical form are acting as such, a group of atoms gathered to develop a certain function with emotions and experiences.

Coming closer to defining the application and function of the Catsanasen method, I would say that this method acts to shorten the distance between energy and the matter that we are, and that it modifies matter according to the new choice of conscious thought that we have decided to create and be. It works directly reaching the most infinitesimal and provoking absolute change, therefore producing the quantum jump between what once was and what now is. Catsanasen is presented in three stages: Beginning, Deepening and Liberation.

Catsanasen means: catalization, healing and ascension in the vibratory frequency of the human being. It acts in all his physical, subtle and multidimensional bodies. Its name derives from the composition of three independent words: CAT for catalysis, SANA for healing («sanacion» in spanish language) and SEN for ascension (here the word has been modified graphically for ease of writing and pronunciation).

When you mentally apply the images on yourself, as an hologram, and you do it with intention and strength and you shape it with your imagination you produce a catalyzation. It is known that a catalyst is an accelerator of chemical processes, so it is widely used in laboratories to accelerate the chemical reactions of the elements, but in this scenario, our chemical accelerator will be the energy produced by the mind in creating the image, which in turn will function as a chemical catalyst where we apply it and accelerate healing, and ultimately will result in the raising of the atomic vibrational frequency of the entire body, producing a molecular healing.

With this method you have the possibility to interrupt the unconscious cycle of repetition that takes place over and over

again, generating an endless loop, and which induces you to live a poor, deprived life of blind suffering. It is not about dominating negative thoughts, habits or behaviour patterns, this is about eliminating them at their very root, elevating ourselves and not generating them any more. The goal of this method is for you to learn to use your intuition and not your mind for self-healing.

GUIDE FOR SELF-HEALING OF THE CATSANASEN METHOD

It is very easy to apply the Catsanasen method. This method is based on choosing a geometric figure (Platonic solids or Archimedean solids) intuitively and applying it to the area of your body that you find or detect to be blocked. It is like on the computer when you copy and paste, but on your side you will have to put more concentration, intention and direction into the mental energy when applying the geometric figure.

In the three stages presented to you: Beginning, Deepening and Liberation, you will see a series of images with an explanatory text. What you have to do is observe the image along the guidelines of the text, then copy and paste with your mental catalyst and allow everything to happen.

Do it with ease, with love. This work is for you, so that you can get to know yourself. The images are represented so you have a fairly broad idea of what is your physical anatomy and your energy anatomy. Look into you, deepen, know yourself, change everything you want about you, improve your everyday life and be happy.

HOW TO ACTIVATE AND RECOVER THE CONNECTION WITH INTUITION

We are naturally intuitive beings, but the structure of thought that governs the third dimension in which we are living and on which this world as we know is based has blocked us from natural connectivity.

The education system and religion have destroyed the natural and magical spiritual connection provided by intuition. The channel through which our higher self speaks and assists us is intuition and it is absolutely necessary to clear it and unclutter it so that the energy can flow freely.

To live guided by a permanent intuitive state will provide you with such confidence and freedom that nothing and nobody can overshadow it. But how do you know if you are

connected to your intuition? The first thing you have to do is analyze and understand how your mind speaks to you. When you observe something and begin to conceptualize, analyze or judge it, it means you are in mind, in ego, in fear. When you allow yourself to observe without analyzing, in a neutral and free state, and being in this state, you make a decision or choose something, it clearly means that you are in vibration and intuition.

To work with Catsanasen's methodology you just need to be connected to your intuition. The first thing we do in the Catsanasen courses is to establish this connection. It is very simple: I instruct the participants to observe the figures of Sacred geometry that you will see in this book later, and that are: the tetrahedron, the icosahedron, the octahedron, the hexahedron, the dodecahedron, the sphere and the spiral. I invite you to let your gaze wander through the images, to allow the figures to show themselves, to express themselves, and in doing so you see that your gaze goes directly to one, you don't understand why, but you have a certainty that this is the one you are going to choose. That certainty is the intuition that is speaking to you, and so there is no mistake, only accuracy. But you must be faithful to this, and pay attention to whether you listen or if, on the contrary, you want to control and look for another figure that goes better with what you think is better.

Remember that the mental system to which you were subjected prepared you to doubt yourself and your divinity because then it would be easier to rule humanity from fear and insecurity. Therefore, your mind will be very used to be governed by reason and analysis, that is, your left hemisphere. That is why the first thing we do is ignore all kinds of analysis and conceptualization, we just observe the images and choose them. Perhaps at the beginning it is a little difficult, but with practice you will see that it will be easy and light to live connected to intuition; I apply it to everything, whether it is to choose one street or another, to choose one menu or another in the restaurant... For example, when I go to the supermarket I stop in front of the fruit and vegetable stand, watch them and let my body intuitively choose the vitamins and minerals it needs,

this way I'm sure I'm eating what I need right now. Or when I have to choose what I wear, the colors tell me what I need. This also applies to work and relationships.

Sensations and emotions will be expressed in your body and if you know how to listen to them, they will speak to you in an intuitive way, which will help you avoid many headaches and unnecessary suffering. Remember that the first impression is the one that counts and it warns you of what may come next.

Listening to the subtle messages of your higher self will keep you awake, intuitive and happy. It is time for this to be the natural state of your mind.

CATSANASEN STAGES

Beginning

In the beginning everything was clear and vibrant, free from the rigid mental structure. This is how «Beginning» was born, independent, easy and clear.

Connected to intuition is how you become a master of Catsanasen's language.

You connect for the first time with the geometric figures from the right hemisphere and discover the different vibrations that the geometric forms present to you. The subtle bodies teach you that there is an energy anatomy that is just as important as the physical anatomy, and that your subtle bodies hold the memories of beliefs, fears, traumas and illnesses that can be your own or inherited and that affect your life and your body within the present you are living. " Beginning " gives you the fundamental basis to understand and integrate this language, you unveil your hidden power, your right hemisphere is activated and your central channel is cleared allowing your sleeping divinity to wake up and express itself in you.

Deepening

The deepest memories that you hold in your body will see the surface and you will go into the densest and most hidden part of yourself so that it can be modified.

It will be difficult, but this is the stepping stone that will take

you to the next vibrational stage.

Applying geometry to muscles and bones, recognizing organs, glands, systems and cells, even discovering parts of your body that you didn't even know existed, will lead you to become aware of what you inhabit, of the physical space in which you stay to fulfill your role as a human being. Discovering your physical anatomy connects you to the matter that you are and from which you generally find yourself disconnected from because your mind and emotions occupy all your attention. "Deepening" is the stage for going deeper into the matter.

Liberation

It's the natural state. It's the ecstasy of the spirit. Happiness rushes into the atoms of your entire body. It is the state of being that vibrates. It is matter and spirit connected by the ether. Knowing your body in depth allows you to be the magician that moves the energy through the main points, which will allow you to reach absolute mastery of your physical, subtle and multidimensional body, traveling with your clear and liberated consciousness inside and outside of you."Liberation" is the stage in which your body is inhabited by your spirit; it is the stage in which you are aware that you can live in heaven while on Earth.

BEGGINING

In this stage we will know the geometric figures, the subtle bodies and, most importantly, we will establish contact with the intuition.

We will be initiated in the language of Catsanasen.

THE FLOWER OF LIFE

1- Catsanasen is born from the flower of life

The first time I heard about the flower of life was during a dream and this is how I usually receive information. A voice that is familiar to me because on other occasions it has spoken to me, simply told me "The Flower of Life", and from then on I began to receive information in images and words that guided me and told me how to apply the information I was receiving to myself.

This image you see here has been found or in different

countries: Ireland, Turkey, England, Israel, Egypt, China, Tibet, Greece, Sweden, Finland, Iceland, Yucatan and Japan. It generally carries the same name, although it has also been found as "the language of silence" or "the language of light", which is what I like to call it best.

The flower of life contains within itself the proportions of every aspect that exists in life, it contains every mathematical formula, every physical law, every harmony of music, every biological form and every atom.

It is called "flower of life" because in addition to resembling a flower at first sight, it represents the cycle of a fruit tree: the seed, the tree, the fruit and the flower. If you want to make this drawing you have to superimpose and rotate the circles that you see here drawn.

(For more information you can search on the internet how to draw the flower of life) But that is not what I am most interested in you learning, but for you to know that these drawings with their circles represent cycles, that they are stages and that they are contained in dimensions that you will understand later through these images. The important thing is that you know that this drawing is in you, so observe it and let it begin to speak to you and to generate a new language of light.

CONNECTION

Connecting with others and interacting can be an easy affair for some and very difficult for others; the same goes for trying to connect with oneself, sometimes it costs more than other times.

Connecting with oneself requires a genuine interest in knowing ourselves, time, and the ability to break through our own mental barriers. Any coaching or therapeutic process has as its priority to help you access more knowledge about yourself. There are also other methods to do this, such as meditation.

But many times the mind goes so fast that it needs to be approached from a place that allows you to enter more easily and directly; you cannot expect your mind to obey and convert to meditation and serenity from one moment to the next. All

the systems used up to now require a lot of time and dedication because the mind has been tried to be approached from the left hemisphere and this delays the process. What I propose with my method is that you enter the depths of your mind and your being from the right hemisphere. This hemisphere will allow you to express, feel, vibrate, and flow with the feminine energy of creation itself. Co-create with the universe in a quantum and spiritual way to live your new material reality.

Below you will see a simple meditation guide to enter a state of greater connection with yourself. I recommend that you apply this meditation on a daily basis until you have it permanently incorporated. This will help you to be in harmony with your mind and at any time you need to choose a figure you can do it spontaneously. Although if you have your own way of connecting, I think it's perfect!, it will be better for you to do it your way, but if you still do not have it here is my proposal.

GUIDE TO ENTRY INTO A NEUTRAL AND MEDITATIVE STATE WITH THE MIND

2- Meditative State

Sit down comfortably and in a nice place for you. Take a slow, deep breath and let the air out. Remain silent inside. Visualize a light that comes down from above, from the cosmos, and that little by little is entering your head and begins to flood your right hemisphere, then the left, the center of the brain, continues down the spine reaching the sacrum, the coccyx, out the hips, and continues down the legs, continues down ... and out the soles of the feet and into the ground.

Mentally check the route you have taken with this light and see if it has been blocked or stopped somewhere. Keep this in mind because here is most likely where you have a blockage to work and you will work on it later as you incorporate this method.

In case this guide is not so easy for you, I propose another one:

Have a seat, relax, make yourself comfortable and start visualizing a small sphere, the size of a ping-pong ball, inside your head in white or blue, choose what you prefer. Put it inside your brain and imagine that it starts to grow from a ping-pong ball to a golf ball, from a golf ball to a tennis ball, from a tennis ball to a soccer ball (but small, the kind used in indoor soccer), and finally, from this soccer ball to a bigger soccer ball that covers the whole head, comes out of the head and surrounds it all as if it were an astronaut's helmet. This expansion of light inside your head will cause all the amount of thoughts and toxins that are generated to come out and be cleaned up.

I invite you to look at image No. 2 and practice meditation.

ACTIVATING THE RIGHT HEMISPHERE AND RECONNECTING IT WITH THE LEFT ONE

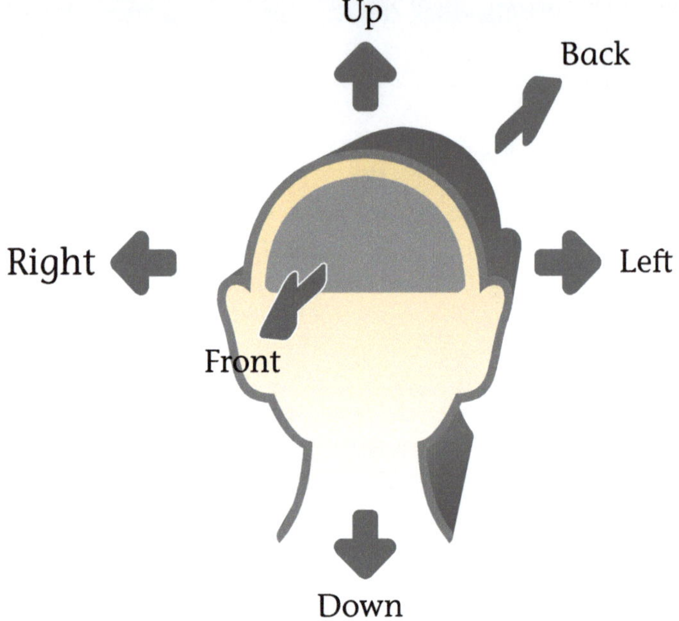

3- Hemisphere activation

After lowering the light in the meditation of the previous exercise and carrying it throughout the body, we will reconnect to this light, but this time focusing it on the brain. First illuminate the whole right hemisphere and imagine how this light slowly pours into the center of the brain, just like a wave of light that goes through the center and begins to flood the left hemisphere. Observe how it is distributed from top to bottom and from bottom to top. It is important to give the order and do the exercise of seeing how the light enters along with the firm intention: from top to bottom, from bottom to top and from left to right, from right to left, from front to back and from back to front, while visualizing with firm intention the interconnection of the areas of the brain with the light.

THREE-DIMENSIONAL GAZE

It is important that you exercise your eyes and their muscularity, as well as your brain, so that this new way of seeing life begins to be known and accepted by your mind. Geometric shapes and their application to your body require a multidimensional look. We all have this ability, but we have forgotten it, a fact that causes our eyes to look only one way and our brain to understand only one plane.

EXERCISES TO SHARPEN THE VISION AN ACTIVATE THE CEREBRAL HEMISPHERES

Place the index finger of your hand about 6 inches from your eyes, focus your gaze on your fingertip, then look behind your finger, at the background behind it, and if you look at any object that may be behind the finger you will notice that you see it double or that you can see through it. In the same position, start looking at your index finger, focusing, defocusing and trying to look at some object that is behind this finger; that is, you focus, defocus, focus and defocus again.

EYE EXERCISES: MOBILIZING THE EYE MUSCLES

Look up, down, left and right. Rotate your eyes clockwise. Look far away, at the horizon. Look all around you without focusing on anything specific. Look at some detail in front of you. Focus and unfocus your gaze on the object.

You can do it as many times as you want, but without getting tired, do it with ease.

SACRED GEOMETRY

Everything in the universe is geometric, anything in the universe can be measured on a geometric scale. Ancient civilizations knew that there is a deeper understanding of the universe, a pattern to everything in existence, even intangible things like emotions, thoughts and music. These simple figures you are seeing are information codes, they are the ones that write the origin of everything you see. It's the software of nature and all of existence. The set of these figures is called: Platonic Solid. Plato, the Greek philosopher, used them the most at that time. These figures belong to ancient and sacred knowledge that has been kept and hidden, and that today is revealed so that we can all live better.

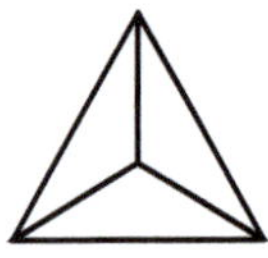

Tetrahedron:
Fire

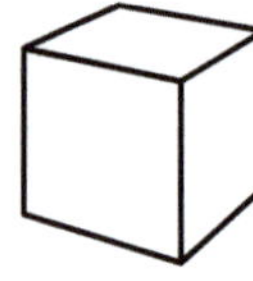

Hexahedron:
Earth

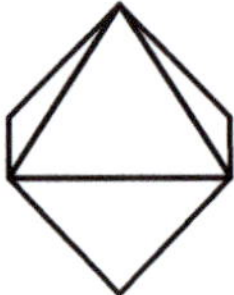

Octahedron:
Wind

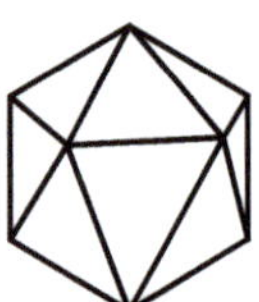

Icosahedron:
Water

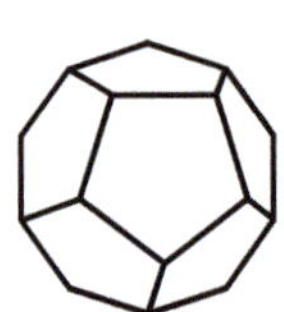

Dodecahedron:
Ether

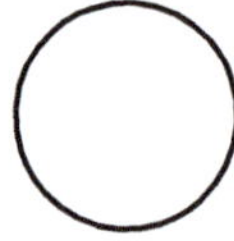

Sphere:
Vacuum

Spiral:
Energy in motion

4- Platonic solids plus sphere and spiral

Now just contemplate the images, let the geometry itself call you, let the vibration of the figure make your eyes look at it and your mind simply feel that sense of certainty that tells you: I don't know why, but this figure is calling me. Don't rationalize anything, forget to consider if a figure is prettier than another, or more complex, or simple, or if this thing I'm or if this thing I'm about to do will really work.Forget all this chatter, doubt and confusion. All this is your ego, your mind, your left hemisphere wanting to control it.

Look at the geometric figures, imagine that you enter with all your subtle bodies (Fig.6) into the figure you have selected (Fig.4). Allow your mind to imagine freely. It is important that you see yourself and sit inside the figure. It may be that you see the images in color, or have the desire that they are of some special color or simply black, grant yourself.

It also allows your mind to see the possibility that the figure can rotate while you are inside. If you feel the need for the figure to rotate, do it, do not limit yourself. It can be in all directions: top to bottom, right to left, bottom to top, or left to right. If you are attracted to more than one figure, it will also be perfect.

Just put one inside the other and you inside, just like those Russian dolls that go one inside the other (Matryoshka doll). It would be like this: you and all your bodies + figure + figure (Fig.5). And you can put more figures, if you feel it is necessary.

DUALITIES WITH PLATONIC SOLIDS

5- Plato's dualities

Here you can see how one and two figures can be combined. Experience the possible combinations for yourself. Also, if you wish, you can choose through your intuition and create new combinations. Practice, experiment and feel.

SUBTLE BODIES

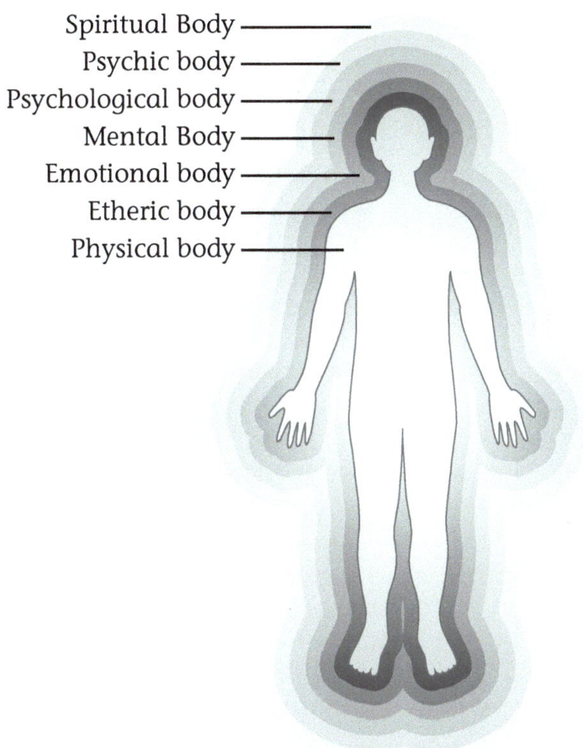

6- Subtle bodies

The image you are seeing here is your physical body with the different layers of subtle bodies; that is, different vibrational levels of your energy, the physical body being the most dense.

At the physical level the immune system protects the body from disease and infection, and at the energetic level, this field you are seeing is the electromagnetic field, also called the aura, and it functions as a protective shield from external influences. The aura is a filter that allows the negative energy that we perceive daily in places, in certain circumstances or

people, to be filtered, controlled and channeled consciously. For this to happen it is necessary to be in harmony because what reflects this electromagnetic field is our physical, psychic, emotional and spiritual state. The matter with which the physical body is made could be considered as light densified in particles. The following layers that cover the physical body are composed of light, which behaves like waves much faster than light, and as they differentiate into different layers they start to become much lighter, thinner or subtler.

So we have a physical body which is the most dense; an etheric body which is the one that immediately follows the physical body and which becomes the energetic template where the physical body sits; followed by the emotional body, the mental body, the psychic body and the spiritual body. It is the bioenergetic fields that are often referred to as the aura of the human being.

The etheric body is an energetic matrix or template where the structure of our physical body is superimposed; this energetic mold is also the vehicle of information that will determine the development of the body. For example, in the fetus during gestation within the womb, as well as that of the structural data that directs the reproduction and reparation of tissues after injury or illness. This intelligent information contained in the etheric matrix is what will give origin to the genetic organization of the cells. There are experiments that show that before the formation of the leaf of a plant, the complete structure of the plant has already been developed in the etheric counterpart. By the same mechanism many diseases have their beginnings in energetic blockages of the etheric body and later manifest as organic pathology of the physical body.

Emotional body: Field of your emotions, which according to the vibration will be more or less dense. The positive emotions will be lighter and the negative ones more dense.

The energy larvae are housed in this body and will be whatever your emotional state is; you will be influenced by these larvae. I advise you to routinely cleanse yourself with sacred geometry to maintain a neutral emotional state for as long as possible.

Mental body: The space of your thoughts will generate a

vibration around you. If you think a lot and in a negative way it will be like a black cloud that travels over you. Information travels as image and thought, these thoughts or egregores can sometimes have color, black being the most negative, and positive thoughts the lightest colors. It is important to check your mental and emotional state when you go to sleep to balance with geometry and not to fall by emotional or mental weight into a dense and dangerous astral plane.

Psychological body: Shows the person's personality. His thoughts, emotions, the education received at school, at home and the influence of culture will give the psychology or personality to the individual.

Psychic body: It connects us telepathically with people and gives us energetic information about objects and places. Our psychic body is the one that perceives, is the one that receives the thought that a person is having about us and brings it to our mind. This is how it happens that suddenly this person calls you on the phone or you call him and says: I was just remembering you.

Spiritual body: It brings the information of all our lives and our ancestors.

It is often fractured by trauma or violent death, and needs to be healed to establish its balance in the current incarnation. You can do a specific work with sacred geometry to heal the spirit.

These bodies are not perfectly shaped as in the image, we have simply placed them like this to give a visual idea to your left hemisphere, which needs to rationalize everything, to understand through a structure.

I invite you to look closely at the physical body and the various layers of the subtle bodies. It is important that your mind begins to accept and recognize the energetic presence of these layers. As you become more familiar, you will detect the energetic blockages in the different layers, but it is important that you observe the image, incorporate it and integrate it into your mind. Do it in a relaxed way.

HOW TO DETECT BLOCKAGES
IN THE SUBTLE BODIES

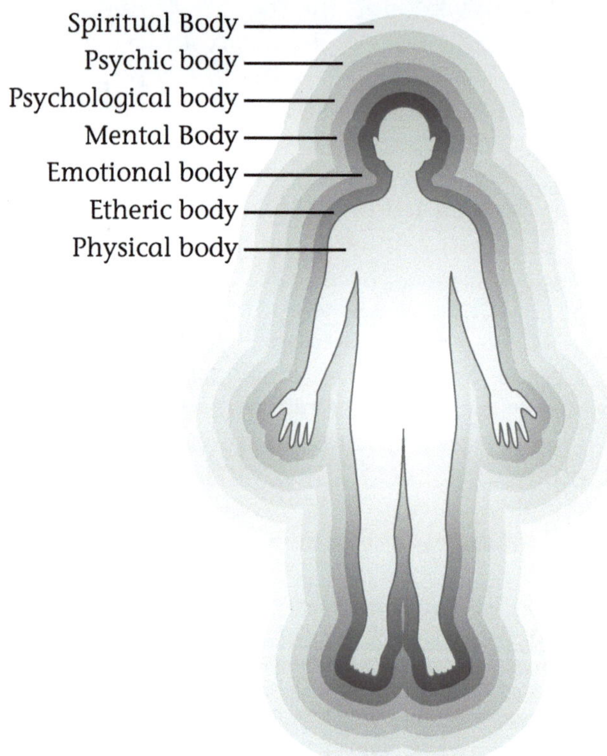

7- How to detect blockages in subtle bodies

Every time you need to connect with your intuition, you have to do the light meditation we did at the beginning: lower the light and leave your mind in a neutral state. Then you have to ask yourself: what I am feeling or what is affecting me, in which body is the blockage located?

We have used again the image number 6 so that on this image you can make a tour with your glance and let it indicate you which is the subtle body that is blocked. As you know, intuition works automatically, you don't need to analyze, understand or rationalize. I invite you to look from top to bottom

and from bottom to top the different bodies and ask yourself the question, in which body is the blockage, and your answer will come automatically.

It is possible that the blockage is in one or more subtle bodies, for example: the physical one with the emotional and the mental one. All right, take note. Or it may be just the physical or just the spiritual, that's fine too. Relax, observe, feel and detect the blockage in your subtle bodies. Take your time.

BODY WITH SPHERE

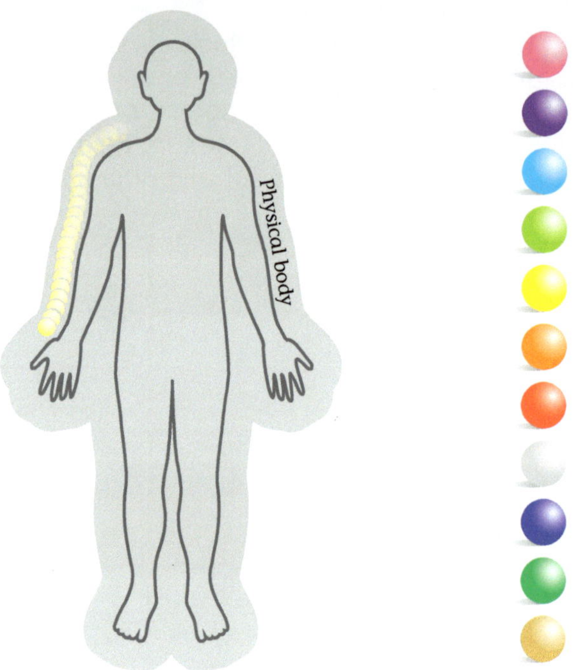

8- Body whith sphere

The sphere is considered "the mother" of the Platonic bodies, symbolizing emptiness and at the same time containing everything. It is the most important female form.

Working with the sphere is something very special. It corresponds to the summary of a channeling that I received long before the channeling of the work with the Sacred geometry. Look at this image where I invite you to use the sphere on your subtle bodies (if you need you can go back to image number 6 to remember the location of the subtle bodies. Now choose, if you wish and need it, a sphere in some color from the ones here and start working the subtle body you think is blocked. It can be the way I invite you to do it in this image or by letting your imagination get its own idea of how to apply the sphere.

You can imagine your whole physical body going into a huge sphere with your subtle bodies, or you can imagine tiny, very small spheres in your various subtle bodies. Allow your imagination, your mind, to expand and create, take your time.

LIST OF THE DIFFERENT LEVELS WITH THEIR CORRESPONDING SPHERE

 **1- For the psychic level:**
Yellow healing energy sphere; clean, healthy and energizing.

 **2-For emotional, psychological and physical levels:**
White healing energy sphere; cleans, heals, balances and connects.

 **3-For physical and psychological level:**
Healing sphere of violet energy; cleans, transmutes and reconnects.

 **4-For the spiritual level:**
Healing sphere of golden energy; cleans, removes, and heals.

 **5-For psychic and psychological level:**
Healing spheres of green energy; reborn, healed and flourished.

 **6-For mental, emotional, physical level (central nervous system, sympathetic and parasympathetic nervous system, enteric nervous system, lymphatic system, circulatory system, energetic system):**
Blue healing energy spheres; refreshes, penetrates and reverses.

 **7-For emotional, physical (heart) and spiritual level:**
Spheres of pink energy that lovingly: clean, eliminate, heal and disengage.

 **8-For physical and psychological levels:**
Ruby red energy spheres; restores, heals and strengthens.

 **9-For spiritual and mental levels:**
Turquoise energy healing sphere; clears, heals and strengthens.

 **10-For psychic, psychological, mental, emotional, spiritual and physical levels:** Healing spheres of orange energy, give strength and hope, stimulate acceptance and grace.

 **11-For quantum cleansing; energy to matter and matter to energy, to other dimensions, unknown places, black holes, dark matter, dark energy, clean the net of networks:** Golden healing energy spheres and all the necessary ones (let intuition guide). They clear, heal and restore.

 **12-Harmonize places:** Spheres of white healing energy and visualize the Om inside the sphere. Harmony inside and outside. Visualize in your body and in the places you want to clean.

The list you are looking here shows the information I received about each sphere and its application; I recommend that you follow this list in the given order.

For example, the yellow sphere you have in the first place I indicate it for the psychic level: "Yellow healing energy sphere; clean, heals and gives energy". Number 2 is indicated for the emotional, psychological and physical level: "Sphere of white healing energy; clean, heals, balances and connects". (If you don't remember the different levels of the subtle bodies I recommend you go back to image number 6.)

Here, in this list, as you will see I am indicating a certain color with a sphere for one level or more levels, therefore, I recommend you to visualize it. I give you an example: look at the number 2, and look at the levels, which in this case are the emotional, psychological and physical. Now you visualize the white sphere and as you visualize the level and the sphere you mentally repeat: "Sphere of white healing energy; clean, heal, balance and link". This is how you have to do the whole list, if you wish you make an item with its corresponding sphere every day.

I would like to make a clarification about sphere number 11, what do you mean by quantum cleansing? It refers to the fact that you are connected to the universe and its infinite possibilities, and every thought that you have, every act that you have performed is impregnated with the universe and its infinite possibilities. Therefore, to finally eliminate a thought or a belief or a blockage is important to take into account that you must go all the way. Repeat exactly as number 11 says: "Quantum cleansing; from energy to matter and from matter to energy, to other dimensions, unknown places, black holes, dark matter, dark energy, clean the network of networks. Use golden healing energy spheres and any others that you feel are necessary and let your intuition guide you to clear, heal and restore". So visualize the dimension of the universe, the infinite possibilities and the golden sphere, or whichever one you desire, that you believe can heal, clear and restore all dimensions. Take your time. Make this list in order, apply it to yourself and choose a sphere each day if you wish, and above all, do it with great ease.

SUBTLE BODIES AND *CHAKRAS*

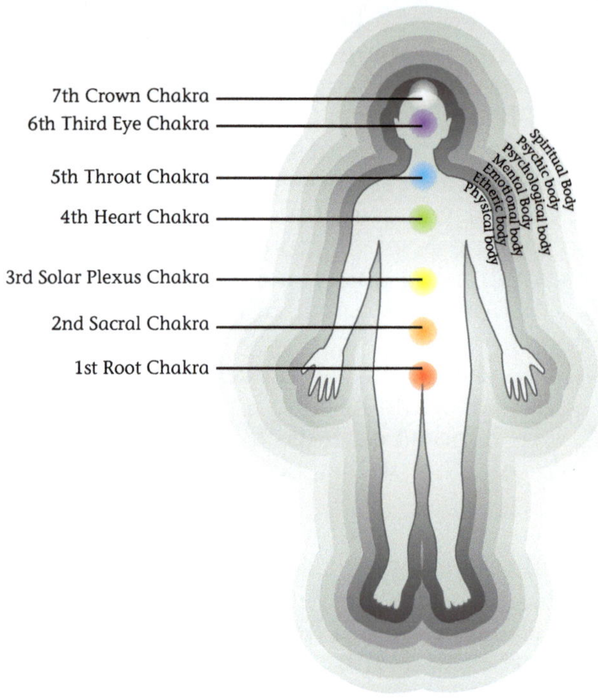

9- Subtle bodies and *chakras*

Chakra means wheel in Sanskrit. *Chakras* are energy centers that receive, regulate and distribute prana or life energy. All the energy that flows through our subtle bodies does so through these energy channels. These centers spread out in a swirling form in the energy field surrounding the physical body and are composed of successive layers of energy that vibrate at increasingly higher frequencies. Each of the *chakras* has a front part in front of your body and a back part that goes behind, as if they were cones, one in front and one behind. Except for the first and last, they are all linked by an energy channel that

runs along the entire spine.

Its main function is to revitalize each aural, energetic or subtle body and with it the physical body, bringing about the development of different aspects of self-awareness, because each *chakra* is related to a specific psychological function.

The first *chakra* is in the coccyx area, the second in the pubic-sacral area, the third in the solar plexus, the fourth in the heart area, the fifth in the throat area, the sixth in the forehead and the seventh in the centre of the crown. All your senses, all your perceptions, all your possible states of cons-ciousness, anything you could experience can be divided into seven categories and each category can be associated with a particular *chakra*.

The *chakras* not only represent parts of the physical body but also specific areas of your consciousness. Emotional trau-ma generates energy blockages causing a dysfunction or de-creased functioning of the *chakras* so then affect your physical body. This method allows you to clean and unblock them im-mediately, harmonizing them in their vibrational frequency. Observe the image and identify the *chakras* in your body and associate them with the subtle and integral bodies.

APPLICATION OF GEOMETRY ON *CHAKRAS*

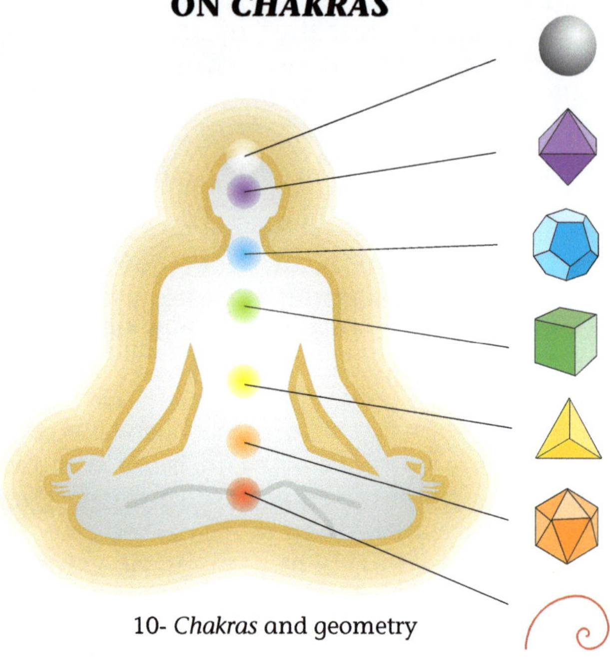

10- *Chakras* and geometry

Sit down comfortably and in a nice place for you. You can also do it lying down, if you wish. Breathe slowly, deeply and freely. Remain silent inside. Visualize the area of the *chakra*, choose the geometric figure that corresponds to it and place it visually in place. Let this figure work energetically releasing the traumatic memories that may be blocking the *chakra*; allow the figure to move, in and out, let it act freely, stay calm and relaxed. You may have feelings or images, do not worry, let it out, just feel. It is also possible that for a few days destabilizing situations happen to you, when it happens it will be good to remember that you have been moving energy, so it is important not to be scared and not to react, just let it happen and everything goes back to its place. I recommend, if you want, you start with the root *chakra* with the spiral rising to the coccyx and continues with the different *chakras* in their order. Apply the figures about 10 minutes and rest. Make one per day if you wish.

APPLICATION OF THE ENERGY SPIRAL

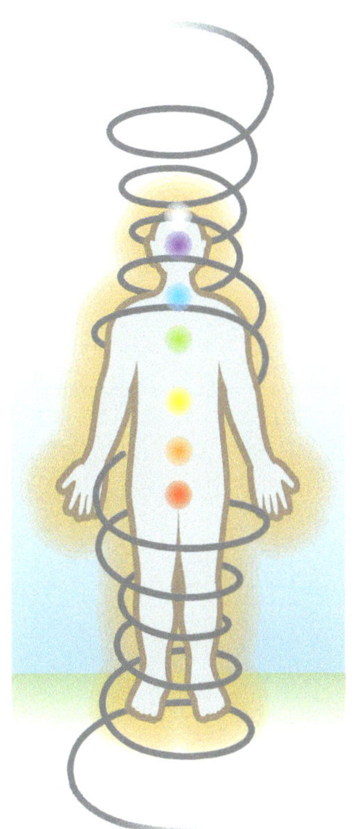

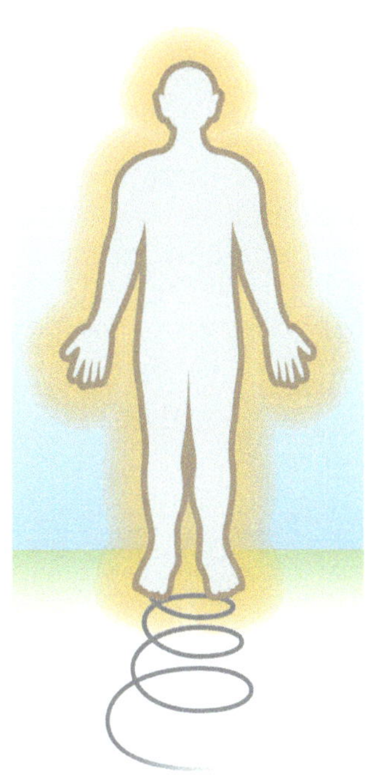

11- The spiral

The spiral is energy in motion, it cleans and removes, and it serves to move into action. I have generally used it as a base to clean and generate movement. Everything moves in a spiral, energy circulates in a spiral. If you feel blocked and see that you are not moving forward in your life I advise you to visualize the situation you are concerned with inside a spiral resolving itself. If you feel numbness in some area of your body at the muscle and bone level you can place spirals and you can also imagine them in the color you want. For the hips you can use images of spirals in the color that your intuition tells you,

although red is usually indicated if you want to move forward.

Sit comfortably and in a pleasant place for you; you can also do this lying down. Breathe slowly, deeply and freely; remain silent inside, allow the spiral to turn clockwise by opening from the inside out. You can also place the spiral on your feet and make it rise visually from your feet upwards if what you need is strength from the ground. But if you need to cleanse your body, the violet spiral will work well from the feet downwards, towards the earth releasing the negative energy

If you have been in front of the computer all day and you feel that there is excess energy in your body, the spiral will also serve to give an outlet to this energy in your energetic body by sending it to the earth, imagine that a big black hole opens up under your feet and this disharmonized energy is eliminated here. Observe the images, choose the spiral that suits you best and allow it to move as she wishes, can be left to right from right to left or simply making circles. Allow the spiral to act.

GEOMETRY GUIDE
IN THE DIFFERENT SUBTLE BODIES

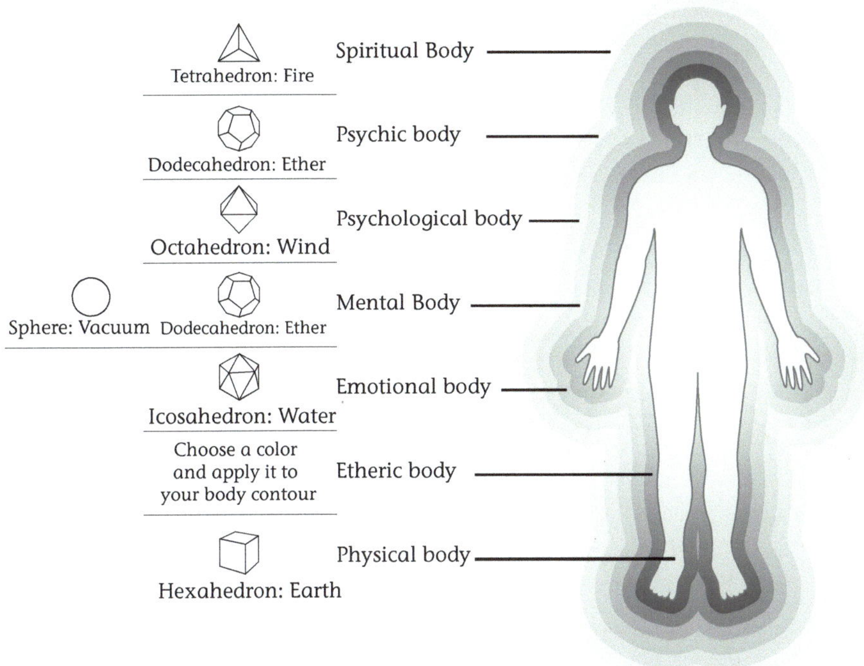

12- Geometry in the different subtle bodies

This is a general guide for you to have a foundation, but you can always have your own experience from your intuition. As you will see in the case of the mental body, I have found that sometimes the sphere is needed to literally generate a vacuum and eliminate excess thought, and at other times the dodecahedron is needed to help you raise the vibration. Always follow the Catsanasen mode to apply the images intuitively, I recommend you to try and write down your own sensations.

TETRAHEDRAL STAR
O *MERKABA*

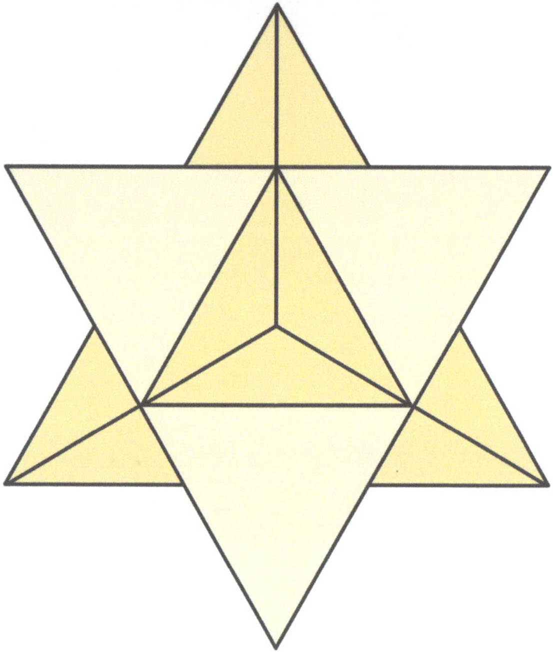

13- *Merkaba*

In this image I invite you to simply observe it in plane, the left hemisphere feels better when there is a structure in plane, observe it for about 3 minutes.

Merkaba means body of light, is the form of your light body, and is also the form that has the consciousness of moving. Activate the star *merkaba* will help you raise your consciousness and expand your heart. It will connect you with the energy of the fifth dimension.

This star tetrahedron is formed by two tetrahedrons, you knew at first when we saw the sacred geometry. The upper tetrahedron looks up and the lower one looks down; these tetrahedrons rotate counter-rotating, that is, the lower one rotates

from left to right (clockwise) and the upper one from right to left. (counterclockwise) Visualizing this star will generate in you the elevation of the vibrational frequency of your atoms; for now it is only necessary that you visualize it as you see it and nothing else. Allow your mind to become familiar with these lines and with this shape, no color is necessary. Simply observe, feel and imagine yourself inside this star.

TETRAHEDRAL STAR
FOR MEN AND WOMEN

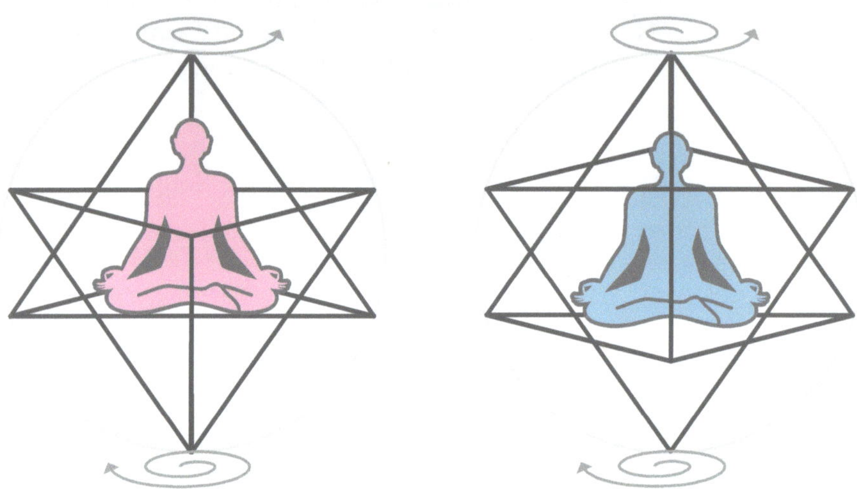

Visualize your *Merkaba*, your tetrahedral star.
If possible, apply this image every day.

14- The Tetrahedral star *Merkaba*

You'll see that we have colored pink for women and blue for men. Having said that, start visualizing the image as it is presented, that is, visualize an upper tetrahedron, a lower tetrahedron and yourself sitting inside both tetrahedra. Take your time, do it quietly. Once you get this image in your mind, pay attention to your body, the middle line of your body, that is, your spine, in it you will imagine a tube through which energy will begin to circulate through a white sphere that goes up and down. While this happens, your star, which is already formed, begins to rotate counter-rotating, that is, the lower tetrahedron will rotate from left to right (clockwise), and the upper tetrahedron will rotate from right to left. This is the same for men and women. Now we have the tetrahedra rotating in counter-ro-

tation and we give the mental order to the star to rotate at a speed of minus nine tenths of the speed of light (270,000km/s)

At this point the sphere that goes up and down the length of the tube stops at the height of your navel and begins to expand sideways and comes out of your star. This expansion is what in the image above you see surrounding the star.

All right, stay steady with this circle around your star and your star inside spinning while you sit in the middle. Feel, perceive, and allow the energy to work.

THE *MERKABA* AND THE CHRISTIC
ENERGY NETWORK

You, with your personal star tetrahedron inside
a dodecahedron and an icosahedron.
Your christic energy network.

15- Your christic energy network

Once you know what your star looks like, whether you are a man or a woman, you have it built in and you have practiced it, you will find it much easier to add two more figures to it. You start sitting comfortably, you create your star with its perfect shape and its tube in the middle, and also the sphere, you feel it, you perceive it, you will achieve this step by step. Once you have done this you allow a dodecahedron to come in size large enough to encompass you and your star; this dodecahedron is presented above and incorporated. Then you allow an icosahedron to come, large enough to hold you, your star, and the dodecahedron. Once you have created the images with your mind, you have seen their shapes and lines well, sit back and

wait for them to work.

If you notice that you find it difficult to create it mentally or to become aware of one image within the other, simply ask them to form and place themselves in the natural order they should go, don't worry, geometric figures know exactly how they should be placed. Do it quietly, enjoy this image. This is the image that generates your light body when you are connected with the Christ energy. Christ energy means the connection with your being of light, your Christ self, your highest possible vibrational frequency for you. Enjoy it, feel how you vibrate in this energy.

DEEPENING

We enter the stage of "Deepening", and as its name indicates, we are going to deepen.

In "Beginning" we saw the energetic body, its energetic anatomy, the subtle bodies, the *chakras*, and most importantly, we became aware of how to work this system of self-healing. Here we will make an introduction and also a brief review of the Archimedean solids, and then we will enter the physical anatomy: structures, systems, organs, tissues, cells; everything that is under the skin that is covering you.

The images are presented in a simple and general way so that your brain can easily adapt and allow you to work better when applying the figures, but you can always consult the physical anatomy in a deeper way on the web.

GEOMETRY, ELEMENTS AND ORGANS THAT ARE RELATED

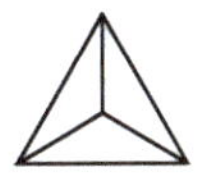 Tetrahedron: Fire	**Tetrahedron:** is related to the element of fire and is related to the stomach. It works on the energy body and with energy making it ascend, it serves to increase energy and vibrations in general. It is also related to the solar plexus, the third *chakra*.
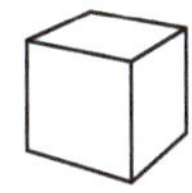 Hexahedron: Earth	**Hexahedron:** relates to the physical and solid, to the earth, and the organ with which it is associated is the heart. The hexahedron serves to store and concentrate energy.
 Octahedron: Wind	**Octahedron:** wind element, related to the lung and the spiritual body, the ideas and the breeze. The octahedron serves to eliminate old programming. You can also use it to clear the house of dense energy by placing it in the corners of the rooms.
 Dodecahedron: Ether	**Dodecahedron:** related to the ether element, to the brain, consciousness and wisdom, it is omnipresent. It serves to link you to a higher guide, helps to connect everything with everyone, connects matter with spirit and raises the vibration.
 Icosahedron: Water	**Icosahedron:** related to the water element, the kidney and the emotional body. It is fluid and changeable, serves to emotionally untie the emotional connections you have had and generate new connections, it cleanses your emotional body, if you have absorbed other people's emotions.

16- Geometry, elements and organs that are related

We begin by looking at this simple chart.

It is a basic guide that gives you some information, but you can always follow your own inner guide and use the geometry you need by applying it to your organs, subtle bodies, or wherever you need or want it most.

ARCHIMEDEAN SOLIDS

Truncated
Tetrahedron

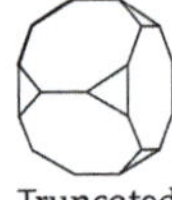

Truncated
Cube

Rhombicuboctahedron

Double
truncated
cube

Great
Rhombicuboctahedron

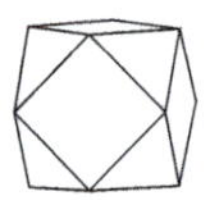

Cuboctahedron

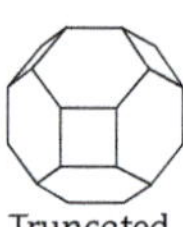

Truncated
Octahedron

Truncated
Dodecahedron

Rhombicosidodecahedron

Double
Truncated
Dodecahedron

Gran
Rombicosidodecaedro

Icosidodecahedron

Truncated
Icosahedron

17- Archimedean Solids

Archimedes was a Greek physicist, engineer, astronomer and mathematician who developed from Platonic's solids this sequence of thirteen solids combined with each other that generate more possibilities of energetic and vibratory connection.

I have noticed that from the spiritual level they produce an immediate regenerating effect, which we will see applied later in the different dimensions. Now I only wish that you observe them and become more familiar with them because they are more complex in image, form and combination. Take your time and observe.

CHAKRAS, SUBTLE BODIES AND ITS DIMENSIONS

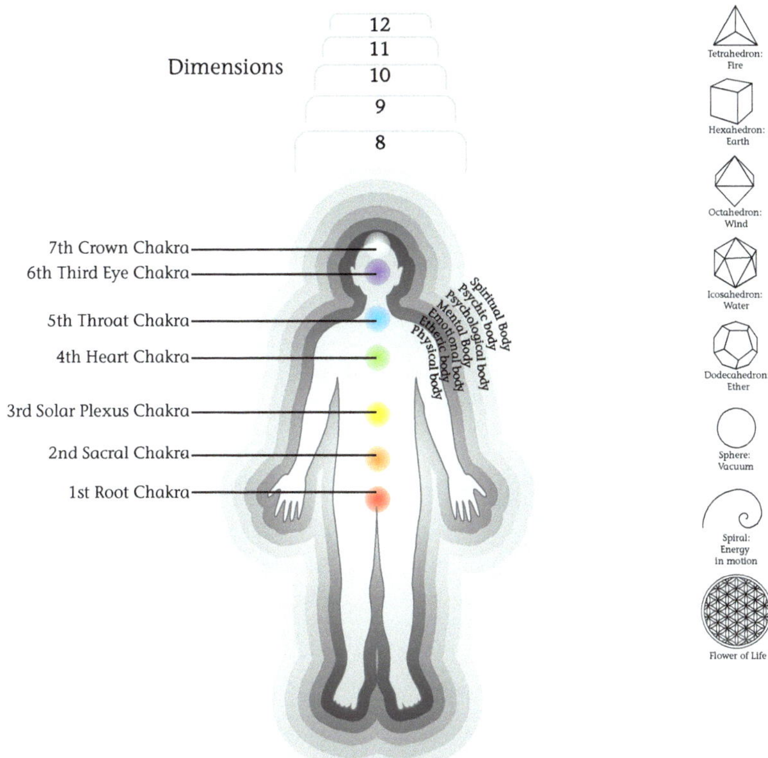

18- *Chakras*, subtle bodies and its dimensions

This image shows you the most important part of your energy field in a rational way so that your left hemisphere can integrate it and understand it, even though in reality it is not exactly this shape, it is just so that you can relate to it in a more -practical way. As you will see in your central part, along the midline of the body the *chakras* are visualized, then, in the form of layers, you have the subtle bodies, and from your spiritual body the dimensions begin, which are states of consciousness (here we have listed them to name them differently than the rest). Observe, integrate it.

ARCHIMEDEAN AND PLATONIC SOLIDS APPLICATION

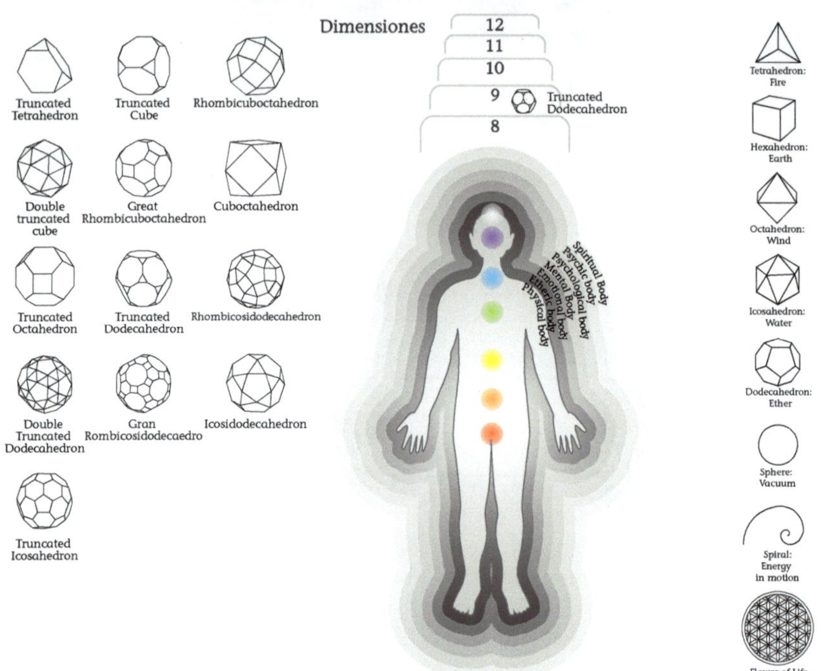

19-Archimedean and platonic solids application

As you have done in the " Beginning " level by applying Platonic solids to your subtle bodies I invite you to experience the application of the Archimedean solids in the dimensions. So, if you want to continue to apply the solids in the subtle bodies, you can do so with Platonic and Archimedean solids in your dimensions. To the right of the image you have Platonic solids exposed, and Archimedean solids on the left of the image, so that you can make a global vision, if you want to use it.

Through your intuition, as taught in the " Beginning " level, select the figure that you think is most convenient and apply it to the body or dimension that you consider to be blocked.Remember to take your time to be neutral and calm, lowering the light, placing yourself in a comfortable and relaxed position and letting your intuition guide you. Do not use your mind, let your intuition guide you and it will be perfect.

ENERGY SYSTEM, *CHAKRAS* AND SUBTLE BODIES

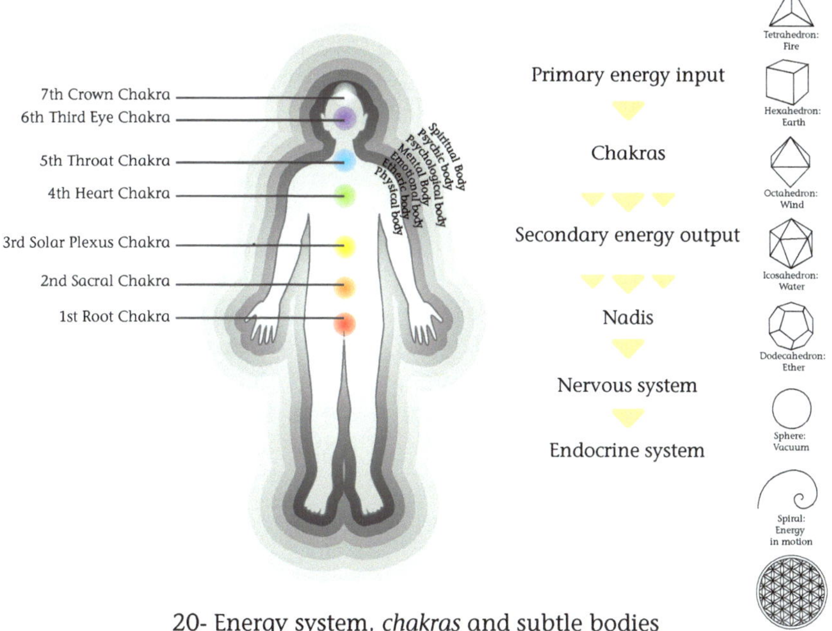

20- Energy system, *chakras* and subtle bodies

This image you see is a comparison between the *chakras*, the subtle bodies and the way your energy is distributed once it enters the body.

It is important that you observe the image and as we have been working detect through your intuition, if there is a blockage in any of the main pathways, for example, in the *chakras* or in the subtle bodies or in the secondary energy zone such as the nadis, nervous system, endocrine system or blood, that is making it difficult to communicate between these energy systems.

How to detect the affected area:

Look at the image, let your intuition guide you, look up and down and where your gaze lands, it will be the area that most attracts your attention and this is where you have the blocka-

ge. What you are going to do next is to intuitively choose a geometry, as we have been working; imagine, for example, the dodecahedron and start applying it to the different areas where you see that you have a blockage. Many times it happens that it is blocked, for example, the throat *chakra*, this will cause that the information does not reach the nervous system, but on the contrary will give the blockage information, which will make your endocrine system (in this case the thyroid gland) also be blocked and not secrete the corresponding hormones. As a consequence, your blood will not carry this energy to the organs and they will start to function poorly.

It is important that you intuitively detect which circuit is blocked and allow the geometry to work. What you will also do in this meditation will be to add the breath and the intention; then, as you breathe in you visualize the geometry, you visualize the connection system you have in this image and you allow the geometry to go through the whole circuit you have drawn in this image. Relax, concentrate, breathe.

NADIS
ENERGY BODY

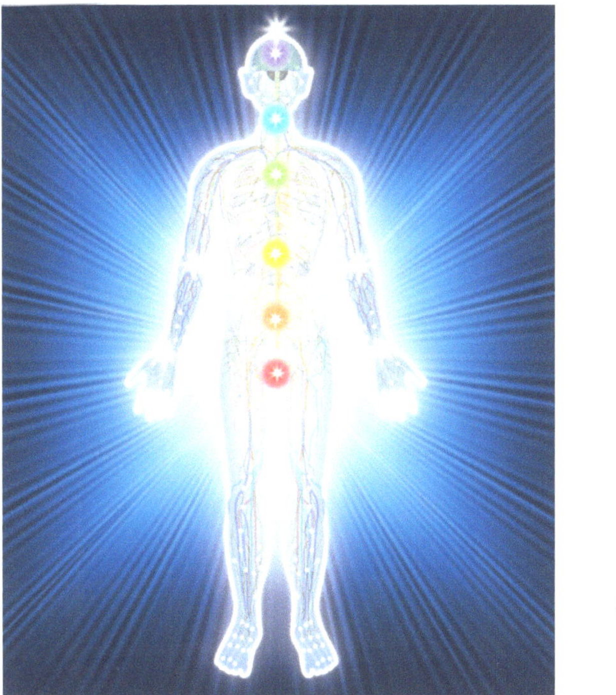

21- Nadis, energy body

The nadis are energetic conduits of bioenergy that communicate the body, mind and your spirit. It is the road through which all information circulates, from how to create a tissue or a cell to how they thought, felt and the experiences that your parents, great-grandparents, ancestors, etc., and also the experiences that you have lived in other lives and the experiences in this one; everything circulates through these etheric conduits in the form of information.

The etheric body is an exact template to your physical body through which this information circulates. Ayurvedic medicine recognizes about 72,000 channels, and in Chinese medicine the meridians are mentioned, which would be the twenty-four most important channels of these nadis.

In the image above we talked about the nadis and how they connect to the nervous system reaching your endocrine system and thus carrying the energy information to your blood. It is important that you observe this image and recognize this energy template in your body, because the nadis are extremely important for the distribution and communication of all your systems. For the health of your organs, tissues, muscles and bones it is important that they are well cleaned because they establish the energy and vital communication between your body, your mind and your spirit, and if any of these are blocked over time it leads to disease.

I invite you to observe this image and draw it mentally on your body recognizing all the space it can occupy, try to visualize if in any part of your body this template cannot be visualized, this means that in that area you are blocked. Breathe, bring your attention to your energy template, detect the blockage and proceed with a geometry previously selected through your intuition, as you learned in the "Home" level. Once selected, take it to work on the affected area, imagine and visualize how it acts energetically. Take your time, relax, breathe, work.

ACUPUNCTURE MERIDIANS

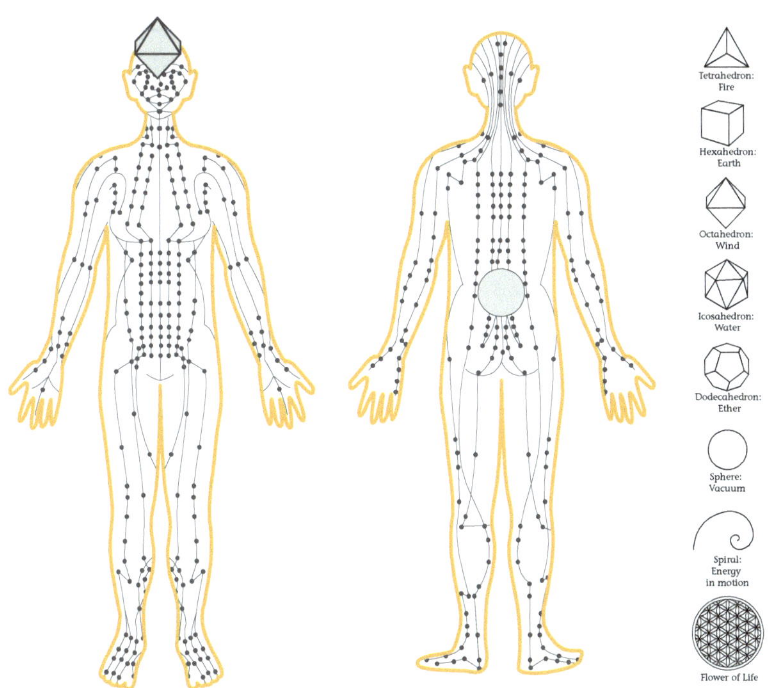

22- Acupuncture Meridians

As we mentioned a moment ago, there are nadis, which is an energetic system of about 72,000 channels through which all the energy circulates with all the information that comes from different places, either from the outside or from within. In the case of the energetic meridians, they are the ones that are going to carry the energy that is produced by the viscera and the organs, and this is where this bioenergy is going to circulate and the meridian is going to distribute it through the tissues throughout the body. The meridians are channels that are found on the surface of the body through which this energy circulates. Dr. Bio Duracu invented the first machine capable of testing these meridians.

There are three types of meridians: the most superficial is

for the tendon-muscular meridians where respiratory energy, defense energy, circulates; then there are the main meridians where nutritional energy circulates; and finally, the so-called "distinct" meridians where hereditary energy circulates. This is where the energetic information of your ancestors is transmitted.

When the fetus is formed in the mother's womb, while information is circulating to create the cells and organs of this baby, the fetus receives information through this meridian from its ancestors and inherits the ancestral energy with the information from the ancestors. This will cause the information of their beliefs, behavior patterns, emotions, lived situations, etc. to appear in your body. This information, without your knowledge, influences your life, your decisions and experiences. In the book "Healing the Family Tree" you will find the necessary meditations to heal these energetic ties. This book is very important to complement your work with sacred geometry.

Acute diseases would be the most recent ones and affect the tendinomuscular meridians, chronic diseases affect the main and deeper meridians.. The meridians are distributed throughout the body and relate the organs with the viscera and externally with all body tissues, which makes them create an integrated whole. It is very important that the meridians do not stagnate (like no other system, of course), but in the case of the meridians it is what once stagnant begins to generate diseases. The main meridians are twelve located on each side of the spine and we can name them as: lung meridian, large intestine, spleen pancreas, stomach, heart, small intestine, bladder, kidney, heart master, triple heater, gallbladder and liver. There are two more meridians that will be seen in the following image and that form a small circulation of energy, they are called "the governing vessel" and "the conception vessel", and they are the ones that maintain the energetic circuit of the great energy circulation.

You can always continue your research on the internet, to get more information you can search: the energy system, acupuncture meridians, and get information about their points, blockages and exact location in the body. As always, what I

offer you with these images is a general idea so that you know how your body is composed and can apply the geometry. Remember that what is not named does not exist. If you yourself do not know that you have energy channels that fulfill certain functions, how can you resolve if you have a blockage? If you do not know your physical body, how do you expect to live on earth happily and fully if you are disconnected from the matter that keeps you here on earth? Remember that you are a materialized spirit living an earthly experience.

It is important that you now observe this image which, even though it does not have much specification, will serve you clearly and precisely so that your mind can detect where your body may be blocked and you can choose the Sacred geometry and apply it, if you need to, to that area, point or line that you see on your body or on the photograph. Remember that you can use Platonic's solids or Archimedean' solids. Take your time, breathe, work calmly.

ACUPUNCTURE MERIDIANS

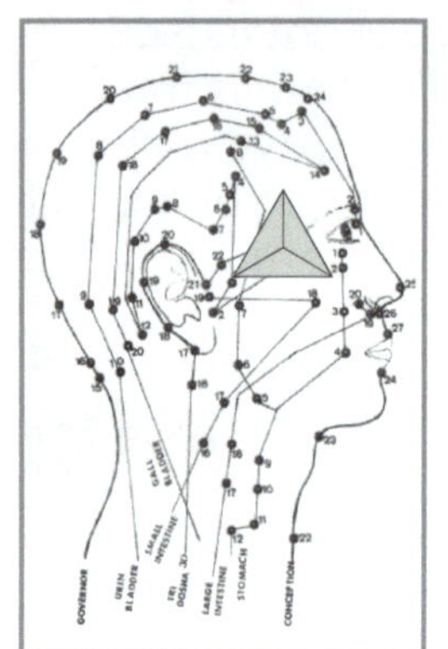

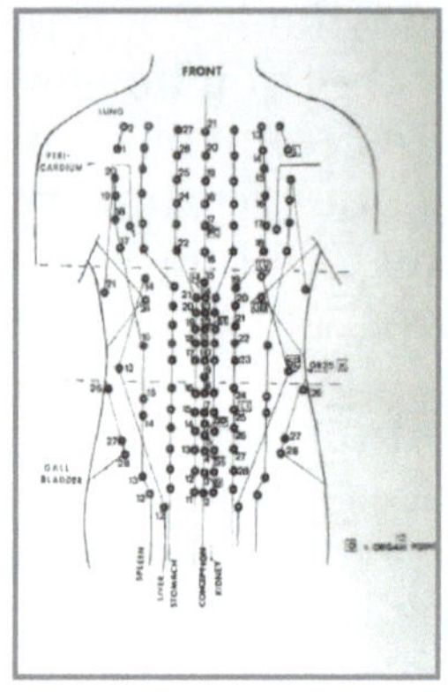

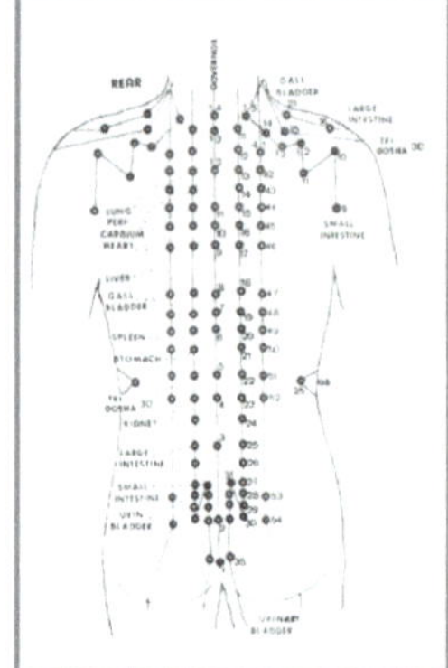

23- Acupuncture Meridians

In this image we show you in a more specific way the meridians of the face and the torso so that you have a wider conscience of the lines that circulate energetically through your body. After you detect where your block is, choose the geometrical figure you feel is the most appropriate to help you unblock and start applying it to the area; simply with your intuition and attention you will give the indicated direction to the geometry in the blocked area and you will order it to start cleaning and working all the affected circuit. Take your time, breathe, work.

MERIDIAN CONCEPTION VESSEL
AND GOVERNOR VESSEL MERIDIAN

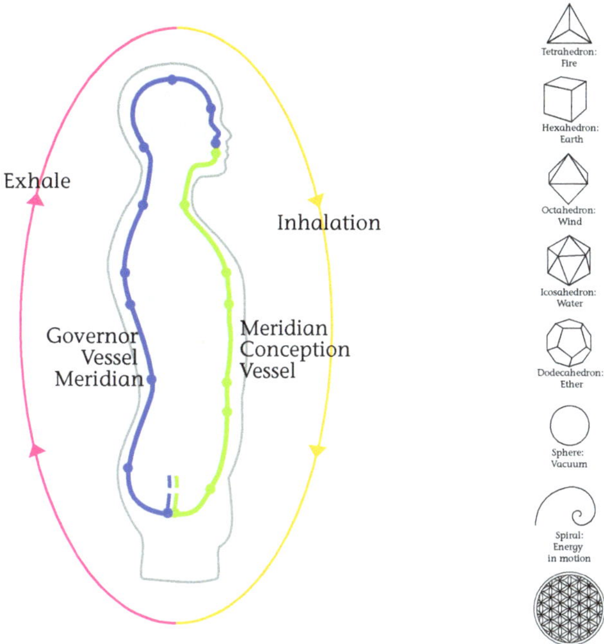

24- Meridian Conception Vessel and Governor Vessel Meridian

As I had commented before, there are two meridians that form a minor circulation: the governing vessel and the conception vessel. What these meridians do is maintain the energetic circuit of the great circulation of meridians. With this image specifically what I want is for you to learn how to do a punctual activation through breathing and geometry. Let us visualize the image and see how the line of the conception vessel meridian (green) passes from the lips, from the mouth downwards, making its way to the perineum, which is the space of muscular tissue found between the genital organs. Now that you have visualized where these meridians circulate through your body, we are going to add the inhalation and exhalation, we are going to inhale and visualize the green line, we are going to exhale and visualize the blue line. If while visualizing and

breathing in and out we notice that the energy is not circulating well or we do not see the line well defined, we are going to choose a Platonic solid, the geometric figures that you have next to the image. Imagine the dodecahedron or if you prefer the sphere and you are going to make the geometry circulate visually through your body, where the line of the meridian would be, cleaning it and freeing it from blockages. Then, this would be like this: you breathe in, imagine the line through your body, place the geometric figure mentally and let it run along the line, reach the perineum, breathe out, and go up with the geometry through the back up following the blue line and reaching below the nose. You make the circuit with your breath and with the geometry on these two meridians. Take your time, synchronize everything, relax and practice.

LYMPHATIC SYSTEM AND
CIRCULATORY SYSTEM

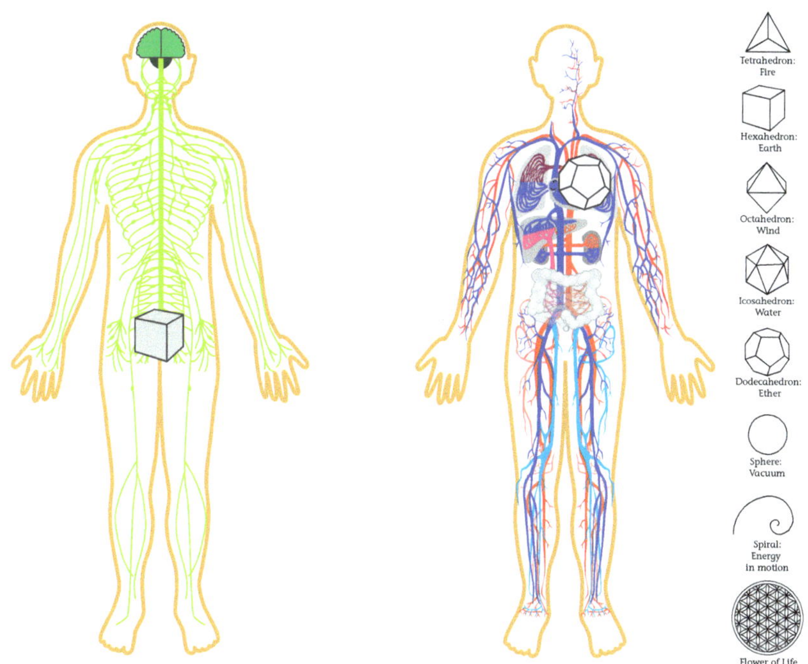

25- Lymphatic system - Circulatory system

The lymphatic system and the nodes are in charge of elimi-nating the toxins that are generated in your body during its normal functioning. For example: with food, with the negative thoughts and emotions that you have daily or with any other activity that your body needs to do and for this it releases to-xins. When it does not work perfectly it generates a lot of pain, stagnation and inflammation.

In the case of fibromyalgia, for example, the pain in the body is generalized, and it comes exactly from a total blockage of the entire lymphatic system; it is important to find the un-derlying emotion that has generated this blockage. Generally, the blockage is usually caused by a belief that was implanted due to a situation or an experience that has paralyzed you, and the mind gets caught up in that belief and begins to gene-

rate an environment according to what it believes.

Beliefs of the kind, for example: - I don't feel capable, or I don't have the power to make a major change in my life, or I don't have the power to change my life at all, I am paralyzed, I don't have the power to do it. These are strongly limiting beliefs.

That means that if your interior is paralyzed, your lymphatic system will be paralyzed and since you cannot eliminate what is left over, eliminate the toxins, great pain is generated in your body. Therefore, it is important that you detect in some way what is the belief that is affecting you and you can unblock it or eliminate it by applying the geometric figure selected according to your intuition, according to what you need to work your lymphatic system as we have been doing. So you choose a geometric figure, visualize the area of the lymphatic system that is affected and apply it mentally. The same thing happens with the circulatory system, but in this case with the blood. The blood circulates through your body in accordance with the ramifications; you will see that there are ramifications in red and others in blue. The red ones correspond to the arteries that carry oxygenated blood and the blue ones to the veins that carry blood with carbon dioxide, some that enter to nourish and others that leave to be purified and freed of toxins. Many times this circulation is also obstructed or blocked by an emotion, but in the case of the circulatory system the one that governs the exchange of circulation is the heart; in it we are going to center the emotions that have to do with love, lack or excess of love. A person who feels that he is not capable of giving love because of the fear of feeling pain will often paralyze his blood circulation.

It is important that you detect the emotion that is blocking your circulatory system and apply the necessary geometry to unblock it. As we have been doing, you detect the geometry and place it in the circulatory circuit that you find blocked. Become conscious, breathe, connect with the emotion that is affecting you, feel it, discover it, bring it to consciousness and give the order to your body to begin to free itself from this toxicity. Breathe, feel.

SKELETAL AND MUSCULAR SYSTEM

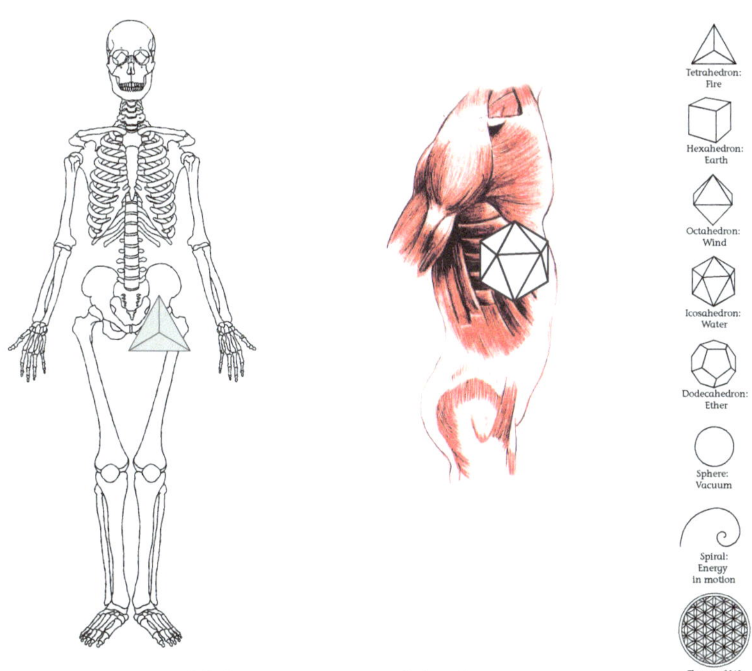

26- Bone structure - Muscles

Here you can also perform your energetic cleaning through Sacred geometry. The most archaic information that we have from our origin until today, the information of the ancestors and the information of everything we have been during the evolution, is recorded in the bones, so the bones are the ones that reserve the oldest information that you have about yourself. It is important for you to know that when you apply geometry to your bones you will really feel changes and sensations in your whole body, so it is better to do it with a lot of tranquility. Also, if you want to go a little deeper, work on the reconstruction of your bones, tissues and muscles; and if this image is not enough for you, you can always consult the internet. The important thing about the images I am offering you is that they are simple, straightforward and very practical so

that your mind knows in a general way what is in your body, you identify it, you recognize it and it serves to apply geometry. If you want to work on your physical body because you have suffered an accident and that bone has been left with information that distorts it or has degraded it in some way, you can do so. It will take you more time, yes, and it is possible that you will have to dedicate 10 or 15 minutes to it every day or two or three times a day, depending a little on the condition you have; but know that you are always working with energy, it may be an energy in denser particles, such as in the bone structure, or in the muscles, but it is still energy and it is absolutely modifiable. So trust, take your time and work on what you need for your body. As always, what you are going to do is detect the area you have affected, choose the geometry that will help most to modify it and mentally apply it in that place and get to the deepest, for example, the smallest part of the bone. (If you investigate a little more you will see that the bone has small cells inside, and the best thing is to know well the ways to apply the geometry).

Take your time, research and make the right application. In the case of the muscles, when you have contractures or injuries, investigate the tendons, ligaments, the insertions, the different fibers and tissues, and the deeper and more specific your idea of what you are working on, the better it will be for you. Research, work, deepen and apply geometry. Give it time to work and you will see the results.

TISSUE TYPES

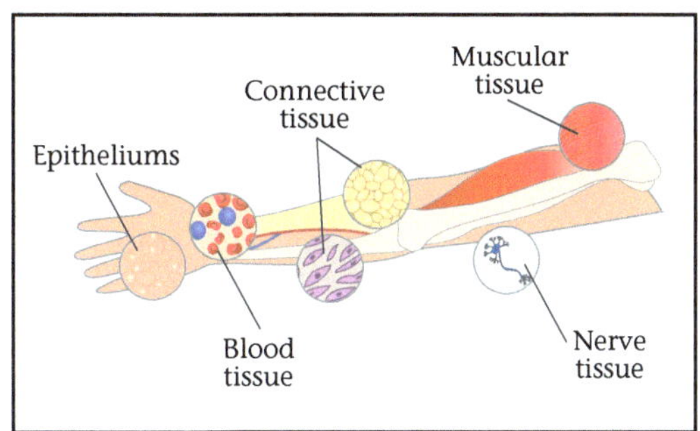

27- Types of tissue

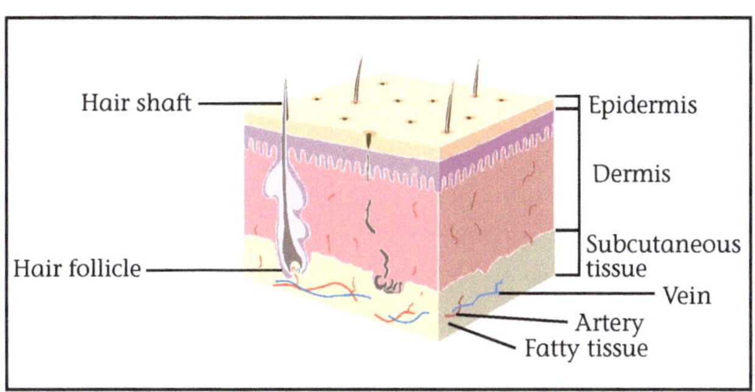

28- Skin

This picture shows you a basic idea of the different types of tissues. If you wish, you can investigate a little more on the Internet and go deeper into your information. As always, the images I put here are mostly to give your mind an idea of the location and apply the geometry. For example, if you have a muscle injury and you look at the picture you will know where to apply the geometry you have chosen, and if you want to work with more precision, look on the internet for the name of the muscle that is affected and it will be much better to apply the geometry. In the image 28 "Skin" different layers are shown with different depths and in case you want to dissolve fat tissue you already know at what level it is.

It is important that your mind registers it so that you can

get there with the geometric figure by feeling the depth of the blockage. This is why it is very important that you activate your right hemisphere and become aware of all your dimensions. Observe the images, detect the blockages and apply the geometry.

APPLICATION OF GEOMETRY FOR BODY AESTHETICS

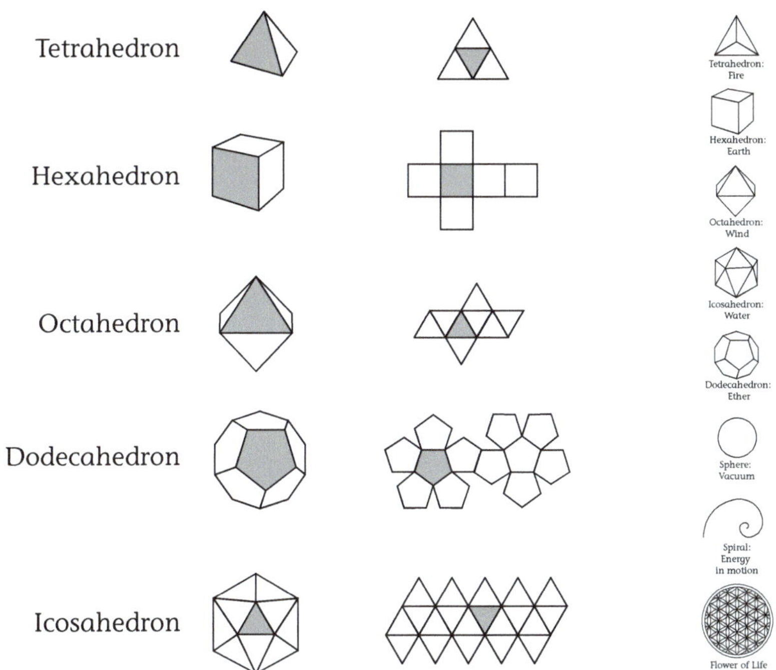

29- Unfolded figures for flat surfaces
(especially for skin, wrinkles, dissolving cellulites and eczemas)

This image is so that your mind can make the relationship of the displayed geometry and can visually cover the flat surfaces. It is ideal to apply on the face, dissolve wrinkles, reach the fatty tissues, cellulite, etc.

Visually generate an energetic maya with the figure you have chosen and visualize it in an unfolded form by applying it to the area that is blocked or that you want to work on, as if it were a fishing net, but this time with the form of geometry that you have chosen and created in light. You can also give it color if you wish. Apply the geometry, relax, enjoy.

BRAIN AND SPINE

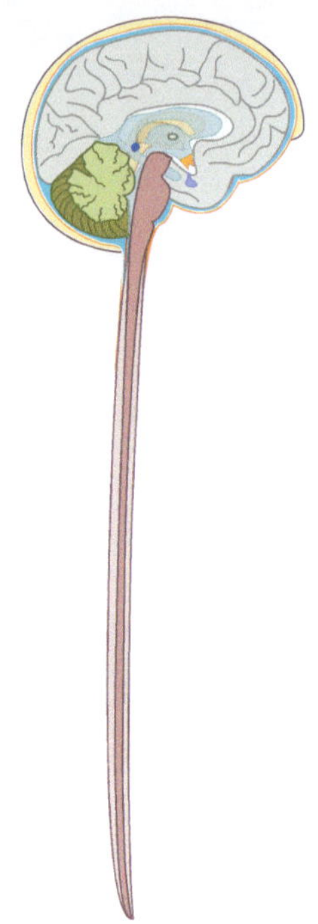
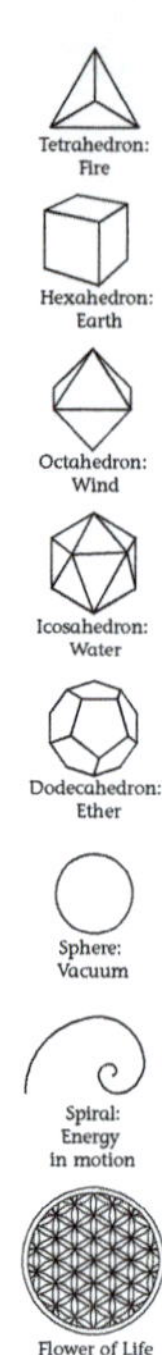

30-Brain and spine

This image is much simpler than what a brain and a marrow is, but it is so that your mind can get used to the shape and you can easily apply the geometry. Look for a day when you are quiet at home and you have time to do a general cleaning and energetic re-accommodation of your marrow. Choose a geometrical figure as we have been doing, visualize your brain, visualize the marrow and start applying the geometry gently. Experiment, relax and practice.

CORPUS CALLOSUM
AND CRANIAL NERVES

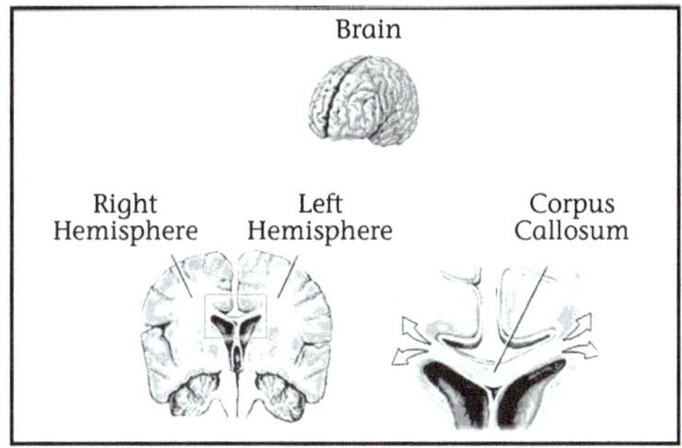

31- Corpus callosum

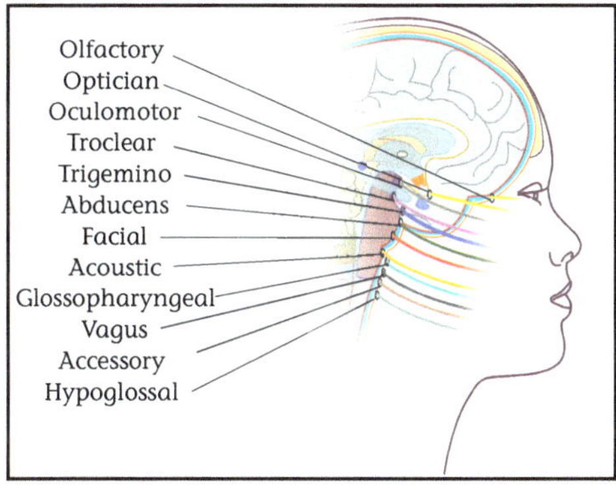

32- Cranial nerves

Two areas of the brain that are important for you to take into account. They are presented in simple images so that you can make an application of the geometry in a general way. Whenever you decide to make a deeper application, investigate a little more on the Internet. I recommend that you visualize the area, choose the figure and apply it gently. Spend only 5 minutes in the application of geometry and rest.

The corpus callosum, among other things, serves to communicate the two hemispheres, so it is very important that you activate the perfect communication between them. Relax, detect the areas, identify the blockage or simply visualize a general cleaning and apply the geometry.

FUNCTIONS OF THE BRAIN'S HEMISPHERES

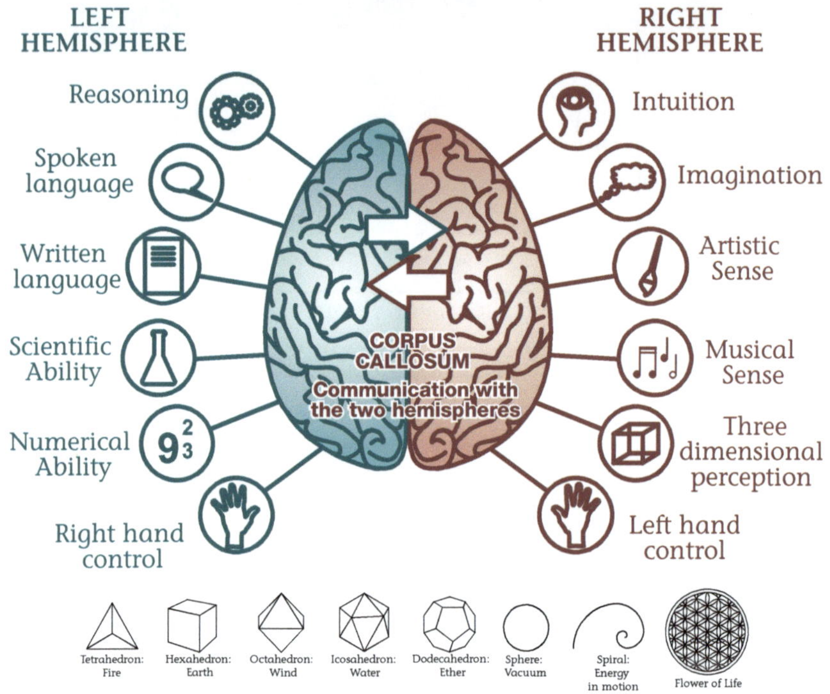

33- Functions of the brain's hemispheres

In this image you can see in a very graphic and easy way the different functions that the right hemisphere and left hemisphere perform. It is simply an informative chart to give you a basic understanding of the hemisphere zones and their functions. Just watch and relax.

BRAIN AND NEURON

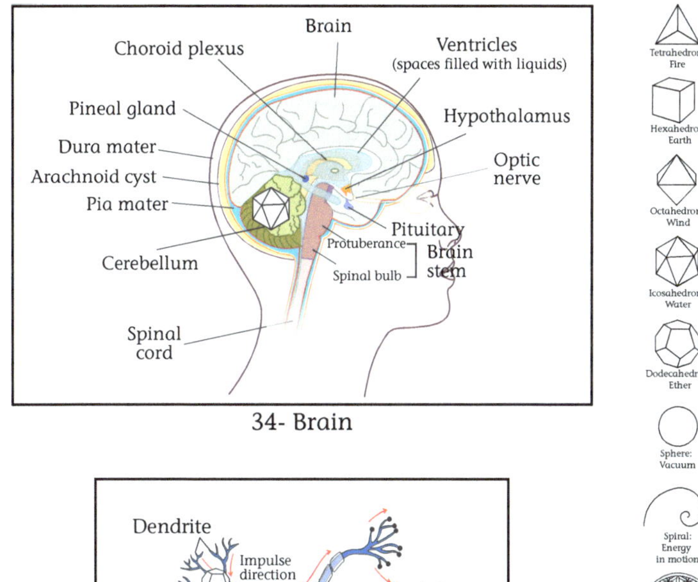

34- Brain

35- Neuron

With these images I want you to know how deep you can go if you want or need to. Dedicate a special time and calmly select the area to work, do not do everything together. Research much more about the brain, the neurons and all your systems, know your brain in depth. Here plenty of information is stored that is currently activated and you do not know, generating many of your daily complications. If you want to work on the beliefs acquired from your birth in your brain, or the misinformation and emotions of your ancestors, I recommend that you go to the occipital area, cerebellum and everything that occupies the back of the brain and start working on them by selecting the geometry that you intuitively feel will help you for that area. Also, if you wish, you can ask yourself the following

type of questions: in what zone is this emotion, this thought or belief that is preventing me from moving forward in my life? The next moment you ask this question, an answer will come, so remain mentally silent and let your intuition answerThe pineal and pituitary glands are very important and you really need to do a cleanse. Dedicate a special day to concentrate on the area and locate it in your body. Do a meditation, concentrate, choose the geometry and start working on the area. I advise you to take that day off for yourself and to relax, to relax, because it is really a place where there is a lot of information stored and it can generate a lot of movement in you and around you. Don't worry, don't be scared, it won't do you any harm, you will just feel energy moving. Do it with peace of mind.

As you can see in the image of the neuron, it has different parts to treat. If you have a problem, a degenerative neuronal disease or illness of the mind, work gently and carefully.

Remember that you can also work this on another person by focusing the geometry on the area of their head, of their brain, where the complication or misinformation may exist. Work gently, with confidence; geometry will always tend to regenerate, to restore perfect order without distortion. Distortion happens because of disinformation or a blockage between the circuits within us, between what I want, desire and what life presents to me. From there all our illnesses arise. It is important that you first discover the cause of the conflict and then apply geometry.

Later on you will find a very simple basis that Catsanasen presents to you so that you can detect the causes more precisely. Simply now, with these images, what I want you to do is to do a general energetic reorganization of your whole physical body and that is what we have been doing in "Deepening".

Continue with your meditation, observe the images and let your intuition lead you to clean, correct or restore what is needed. Continue.

HEMISPHERES AND GEOMETRY

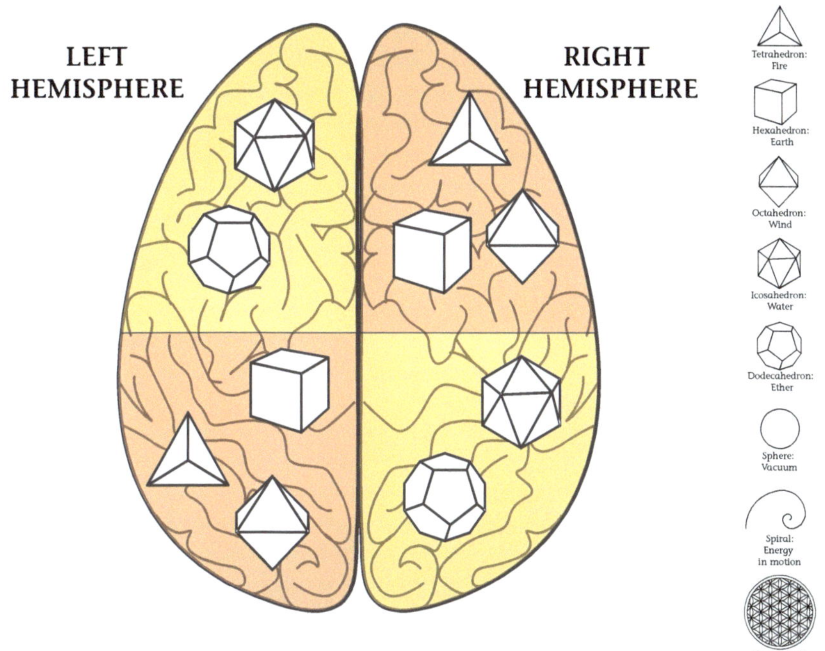

36- Hemispheres and Geometry

In this image you have to apply the geometry as you see it in the drawing; do it calmly, it is a matter of working it in mirror. It is important that you know that this geometry will bring to you an absolute and true mirror connection between the two hemispheres.

You will apply an icosahedron and a dodecahedron in your left hemisphere, in the front, and you will apply the same icosahedron and dodecahedron in your right hemisphere, in the back. In the front part of your right hemisphere you will apply a tetrahedron, an octahedron and a hexahedron, and you will do the same in the back part of your left hemisphere. You do it in mirror and at the same time.

How do we do this? First start visualizing a geometry in one of the hemispheres, in front and behind, start slowly, in parts,

don't try to do everything together. There will come a time when you will be able to have your brain well visualized and determined and you will be able to draw a middle line that divides left and right, and a horizontal line that divides front and back. Mentally, you separate the brain in this way, in four parts, and you place the figures as they are seen in this image; by doing it in this way you generate this dynamic movement of reconnection between hemispheres working it in mirror. It is important that you do it with tranquility and time. You may feel some sensation, don't be afraid we are reconnecting the hemispheres, working with the figures and the forms. Do it quietly, do your meditation, connect and relax.

SYMPATHETIC AND PARASYMPATHETIC NERVOUS SYSTEM

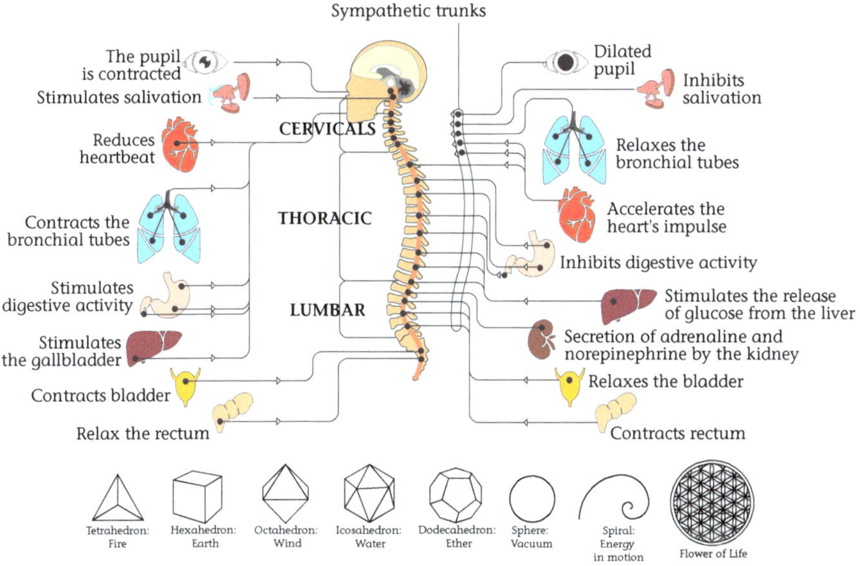

37-Sympathetic And Parasympathetic
Nervous System

In this image your sympathetic and parasympathetic nervous system are presented. I also recommend that you research your autonomic nervous system and your central nervous system on the Internet, since it is very important to know our nervous system in depth. Here we simply present images so that you can see the importance that the sympathetic and parasympathetic systems have in the functions of the organs and about the sympathetic nodes.

As in everything we have been working on, if you feel that there is some area that calls your attention and you see that it may be blocked in some way, and in your body you notice that this organ is affected, what I want with this image is to show you that you can also work energetically through the geometry of your nervous system.

Just as you have been doing, you select your geometry, detect the affected area and apply it. Meditate, connect and work.

ENDOCRINE SYSTEM GLANDS

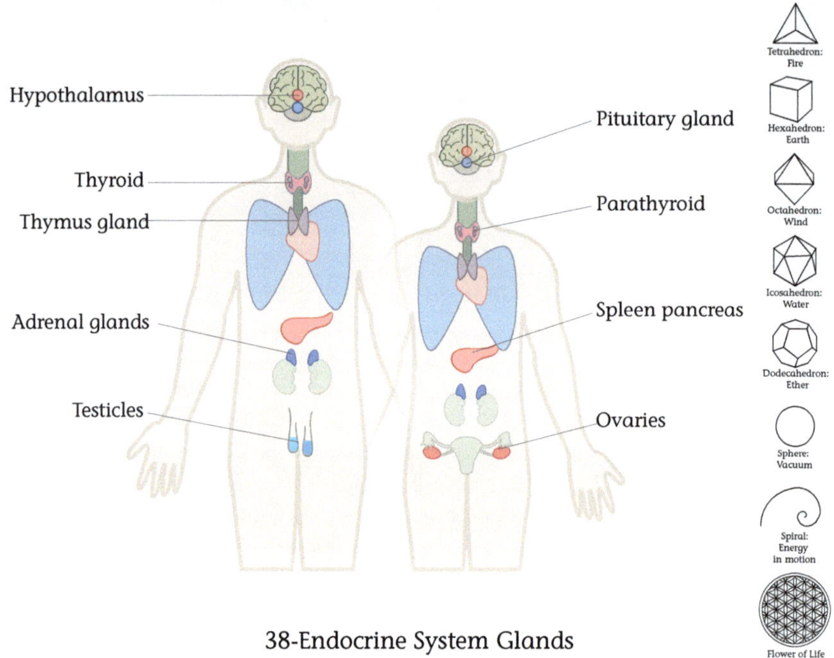

38-Endocrine System Glands

This image shows the glands that belong to your endocrine system.

What I'm trying to do is get you to do a general cleansing or rearrangement of all your glands. As you will remember, we have seen before (in image 20), that through the *chakra* the main energies enter and then they are divided by the nadis into secondary energies and they pass to the different systems: nervous system, endocrine system and circulatory system (the blood), so it is very important that the glands work perfectly so that the energy that has to be distributed by your body can really do it. Negative emotions, traumas, fears, cause diseases or blockages in certain glands, for example, in the thyroid causing you hypothyroidism or hyperthyroidism, in the case of the thymus gland, will give a depression in your immune system and generate that you have few defenses. In the case of

the pancreas, when it is blocked it will generate diabetes. And so with the different glands you can always investigate and get more information about their physiology on the internet to understand a little bit more.

What I propose here is that you do a work with all your glands or, if you prefer, do it in only one gland because you notice that you have only one blocked; although I always recommend a general work to balance all your endocrine system. As I explained before, from your intuition you choose a geometry (the example you see in the image is something optional, explanatory, demonstrative, nothing more), and once you choose the geometry you apply it in the area to work, like copying and pasting in the computer. Meditate, relax, connect and apply your geometry.

THE SPHENOID BONE

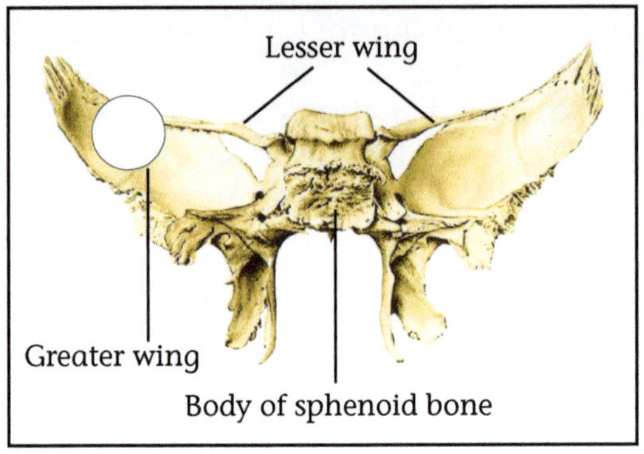

39- The sphenoid bone

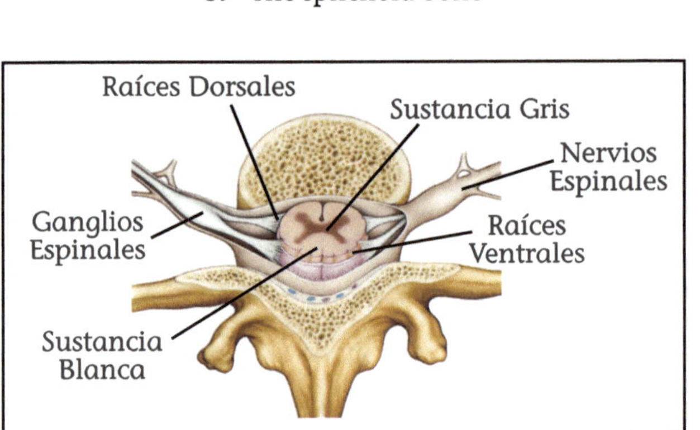

40- Spinal cord

This bone is very important that you work on it and activate it energetically. It is located in the middle of your head, in your skull, or rather, it is where the pituitary gland rests in its central part. That place is anatomically called the "Turkish chair".

This bone is very involved in all our evolution because it contains archaic information, from our structural beginnings until today. Applying geometry to this bony body of our head will generate the activation and energetic liberation of this archaic information, so I recommend that, first, after meditation, you investigate it, detect it and locate it, and once you have located it, do a self-scan with your inner look.

If you need it, you can go to the internet and look for images that show a sagittal or transversal cut of the head, so you can better locate where it is and start spending some time on it, free of external concerns, and you can work delicately on the whole area. You can choose the geometry that your intuition tells you and start working, in this case I have used a sphere. Choose one or two, practice with one and then try the other, but it is important that the wings of this bone called "Lesser wings" and " Greater wings" are activated and move vibrationally. Take your time, do it relaxed. Meditate, work and experiment.

In the case of the photograph below, the one of the spinal cord, it is also very important and that is why I have put them together. These are two areas that need to be worked on carefully, investigated and geometrically applied gently. This is the inner part of the spine (previously we had worked on the outer part) and here you go a little deeper, which requires that when you do the meditation you feel comfortable, know what is inside your spine and know where to apply it.   Remember that what is not named does not exist. Now you have a mental image of what your marrow looks like on the inside. If you know what it looks like, you can apply the geometry. It also shows around the marrow, the bone of the vertebrae; that's what the inside of your bones is like, little squares (I think I mentioned this before, which is why the spheroid bone inside it also has these little squares). Through these small cells you see in the bone pass nutrients, information, nutritive substances to feed this bone and, of course, all your history; in these bones is housed all the most archaic information, as I told you a moment ago, of all your evolution. It is important that with the geometry you work within this to give you this new lighter vibrational information and to activate your new being.

Work relaxed, experiment, meditate, feel.

CEREBRAL FALX

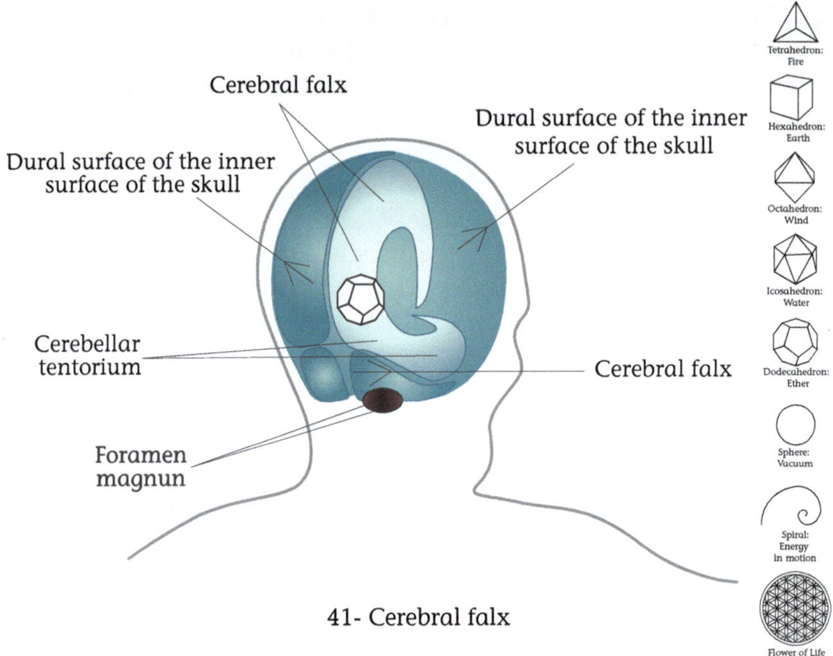

41- Cerebral falx

The Cerebral Falx is a vertical membrane that separates right and left hemispheres internally. Visualize this image very well to be able to work with the geometry. In the previous image we have seen the division of the brain into left and right hemisphere from the outside, this is an internal vision where you will see different parts of this membrane marked. Work little by little with geometry, making an energetic rearrangement of the different parts or spaces, so to speak, into which your skull is divided through the Cerebral Falx

Of the Brain. Do it with tranquility, use the selected geometry with your intuition, experiment, feel, reconnect.

SPINAL COLUMN

Region	Vertebra
Head, scalp, facial bones, brain, inner and middle ear, sympathetic nervous system.	1C
Optic nerves, auditory nerves, breasts.	2C
Trifacial nerve, neuralgia	3C
Nose, lips, mouth, eustachian tube	4C
Vocal cords, neck glands, pharynx	5C
Neck muscles, torticollis, amygdala, shoulders.	6C
Thyroid gland, shoulder bag, elbows	7C
Arms: elbow and underneath, including hands, wrists and fingers: also esophagus and trachea	1T
Heart, including its valve and pericardium: also coronary arteries, functional conditions of the heart	2T
Lungs, bronchial tubes, pleura, thorax, chest	3T
Gallbladder and bile duct	4T
Solar plexus liver and blood	5T
Stomach	6T
Pancreas, duodenum	7T
Spleen	8T
Adrenal and suprarenal	9T
Kidneys	10T
Kidneys, ureter.	11T
Small intestine, fallopian tubes, lymphatic circulation	12T
Large intestine or colon, inguinal	1L
Appendix, abdomen, upper leg, cecum	2L
Sexual organs, bladder, knees	3L
Prostate gland, inner back muscle, sciatic nerve	4L
Inner thigh, ankles, feet, fingers, arches	5L
Hip bone, buttocks	Sacrum
Rectum, anus	Coccyx

42- Spinal column

In this image you have a comparison of the vertebrae and the region it affects, so you also have to consider the sympathetic and parasympathetic nerves that pass through these vertebrae (which we have seen in image 19).

Go back, collect the data, check again the organs that affect the different nerves and compare it with this picture where you have the vertebrae through which the nerves that will affect the different organs pass.

It is important that, through this very simple base of anatomy that I am offering you, you know minimally how your body is composed so that you enter into a deeper communica-

tion with it and that you are not so unfamiliar with any of its parts. The more you know about your body, the better the work with sacred geometry will be, the better the application will be, deeper and with better results; So look carefully at this image and everything that is exposed here, recognize it in your body, do your inner look self-scan, detect what part of your spine is blocked, relate it to the area that is affected and remember that the emotions that have made you feel unsupported by life or overloaded with responsibilities, will affect areas of your spine, which will affect all your organs and all your nerves. Do your meditation, detect the main emotion, find the affected area and apply the geometry. Take your time, do it with love, you are working on yourself, you are re-educating yourself, you are getting to know yourself.

GEOMETRY APPLICATION GUIDE

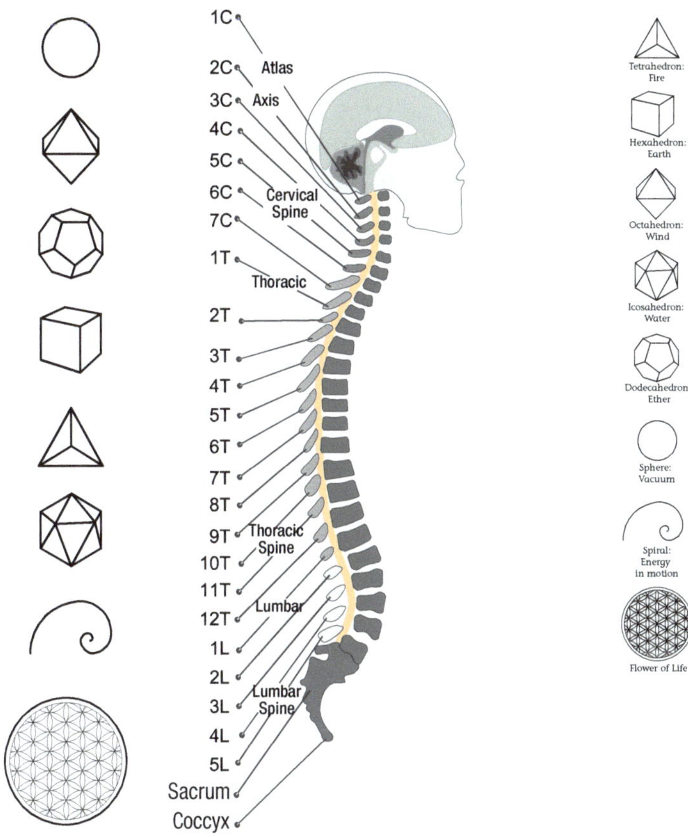

43- Geometry application guide for the spine

Here is another image of the spine, but in this case with a suggestion of application in geometry and regions.

As always, I will tell you to choose the geometry that your intuition dictates or in the case that it is perfect as you see it in the image, apply it. You start one by one, choose a region, apply the geometry, rest a bit and choose another region. Remember that working on the bone system will always generate very deep movements in your whole body, in your whole be-

ing, because we are working with the oldest information you have about yourself, so do it patiently, calmly and slowly.

If you wish you can apply only one geometric figure, the one you have chosen, and you intend to work on your whole spine, dedicate a day to this application; or choose by regions and apply it in those areas. Do it to your liking, make your choice with tranquility; always meditate first, be sure to look for your neutral state when you ask the question "which geometry is best for this situation in my vertebrae", and choose the geometry. Dedicate 5 minutes to the application, let go, relax and continue your day with tranquility.

CELLS, THEIR COMPONENTS AND DNA

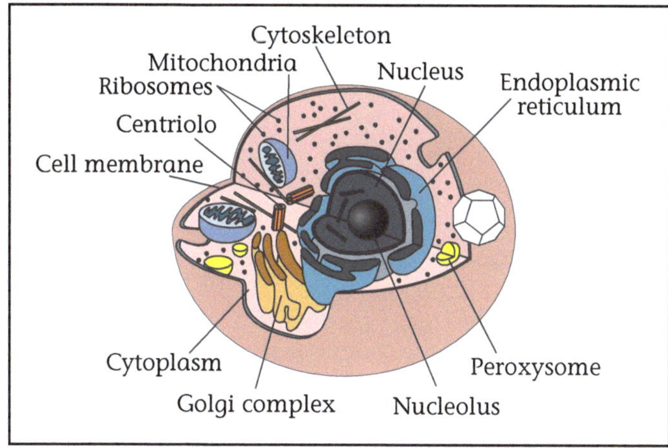

44- Cells, their components

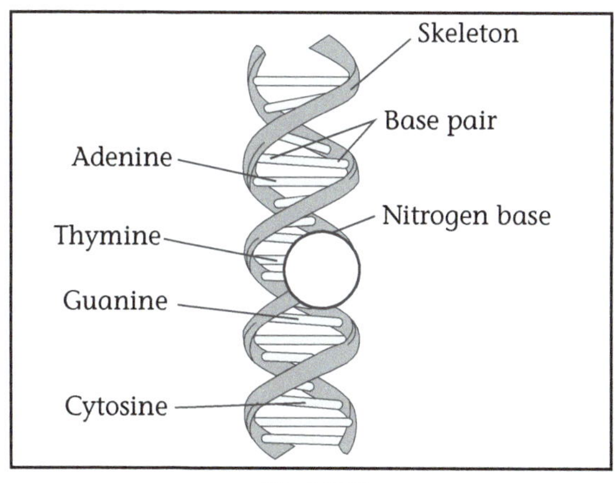

45- ADN

We have reached one of the smallest portions of our body because from here we already enter molecules and atoms.

I am interested that through these images you get to know in a graphic, funny and easy way the components of the cell, the form that presents the DNA and its proteins. The emotions that generate realities in which your life is currently manifes-

ted, many times are housed inside the cells, in the nucleus, in the DNA or in the cytoplasm of the cell, are emotions, beliefs, embedded experiences, belonging to past lives or acquired by ancestral energy inheritance. This information passes through the energetic channels of body bioenergy that is transmitted from life to life by your spirit or through ancestral energetic inheritance by the energetic meridians carrying the initial information that creates the fetus. This energy is transmitted by the mother through the uterus and will give form to the embryo; although it may seem strange, the information will remain inside you, in your first cells, and these will begin to divide giving rise to the different parts of your body.

Throughout your life you will live experiences that depending on their intensity can activate, as a trigger, the information stored in your cells from past lives or from your ancestors.

The membrane of the cells works like a light switch: it will be turned off and for some important event it will be turned on, it will be activated, and you will begin to live experiences or to generate situations in your life, like those that your ancestors have lived and you will not understand why.

Although it may seem strange, once you have the image and you have identified it mentally you will be able to work the area that is affected, even if it is as small as the interior of the cell. It is important that you know these little things about your body, so to speak, because by being aware of this you will be able to choose the geometry and know where to apply it. Remember that what is not named does not exist. If you need to acquire more information about the components of the DNA cell I recommend that you investigate deeply on the internet and learn more about its forms, elements and subelements.

In this book, I present you the basics so you can get an idea, detect the geometry and make the application. In spite of all the journey we have made so far, I will tell you that it is only a small idea of basic anatomy, search more, investigate more, know your body which is where you live, the thinking being, the one who is afraid, the one who is excited, the one who is happy, lives inside this body that we have traveled in depth.

What we are doing is learning to reorganize ourselves, to

decode and understand the emotions that we have, to grow and evolve thanks to the diseases, to recognize in our body the different energetic and emotional blockages and to heal them. It is important that we take care of ourselves and that we heal ourselves from the outside in and from the inside out. Therefore, recognize your smaller portions and have them present every day in your body, in your mind. Even if you are working, cooking or walking, remember that there are parts in your body, like the cells that are active, that are activated in certain situations and that are going to generate an important movement in you and in your body physiology, that are going to respond to a situation, in a certain way. That is why it is very important that you know your inner self, your anatomy and that you know where you live. Meditate, integrate all this, apply your geometry, rest, live happily, free of fears and conditioning that prevent you from connecting with your true and absolute total being.

LIBERATION

In this stage we are going to free ourselves from the limitations of the mind.

We will connect our inner feminine and masculine energy and become aware of the power our sexual energy has to create the life we desire.

A COMPARISON: GEOMETRY
AND CELL DIVISION

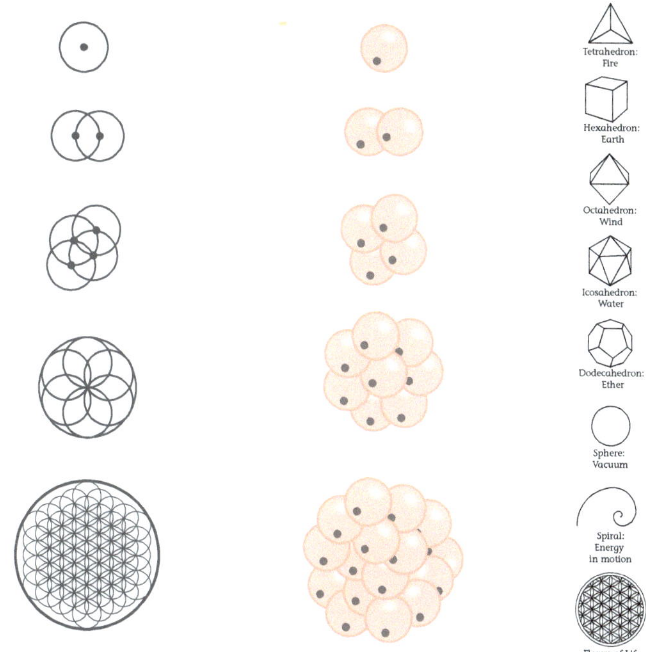

46- A Comparison: geometry and cell division

This image presents a comparison between the cell division that occurs from fertilization and the different stages of the flower of life. There is an unique whole that expands to give creation and evolution.

The flower of life represents the creation of the whole. In its form it contains the code that stores the information of life in the universe and in some way it is shown here as the eternal and ever constant energy that propagates, divides and expands, realizes and creates different forms.

For example, in the human body, from cell division, tissues, bones, muscles, organs, etc. are created; in the universe, galaxies and planets are created.

The two columns show life in motion. The exact proportions in which they are divided and generate all these holo-

graphic patterns created by Sacred geometry, perfect and continuous, lead us always to the same thing: the creation of life that manifests itself.

Observe, integrate and let your mind absorb this information.

STAGES OF THE FLOWER OF LIFE

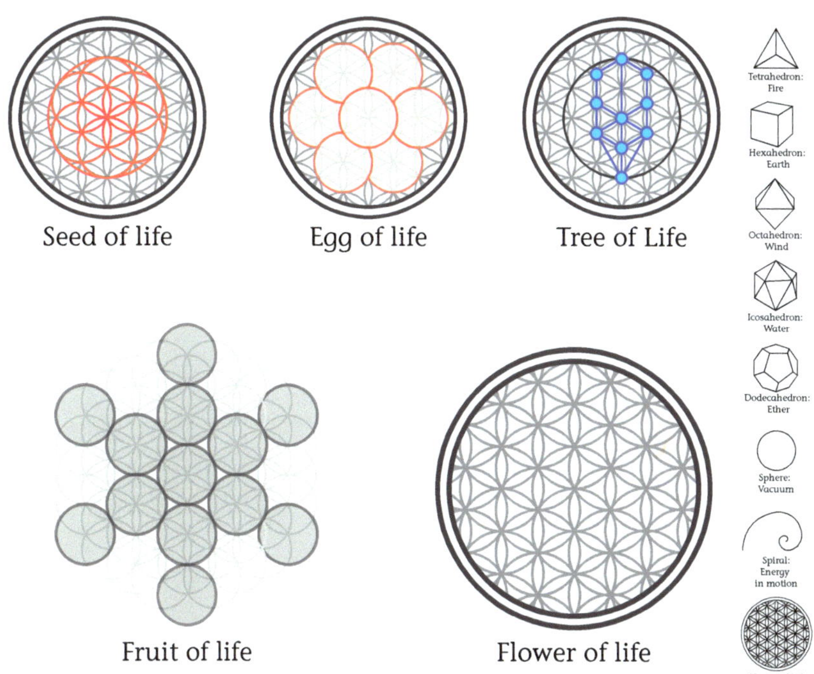

47- Stages of the flower of life

All this knowledge, to be transmitted, needed a proper language and nothing better than an analogical, synthetic and symbolic language; therefore, a code was needed to gather in one place the laws of something. "The Secret Code of Self-Healing" is the title of this book because it was thus pronounced to me in a very clear and direct voice; at that moment I knew I had to expand the information I was receiving.

I felt that it was the same energy of creation that was guiding me through the codes of sacred geometry to decipher the language I needed to learn and integrate and then transmit all the information in an easy and direct way, as it had never been transmitted before, because for a long time it had remained hidden and limited to a certain elite. Now it is time to release it.

In the stages of the flower of life, the seed of life, the egg of

life, the tree of life and the fruit of life are presented. Four stages generate a fifth stage, which at the same time is the stage to be the flower of life. It is for this reason that Catsanasen is born from the flower of life and its mission is to be the seed of light that will give the beginning of the eternal movement of the new language.

Observe it, feel it, and let it integrate itself into you little by little.

ANATOMICAL PROPORTION

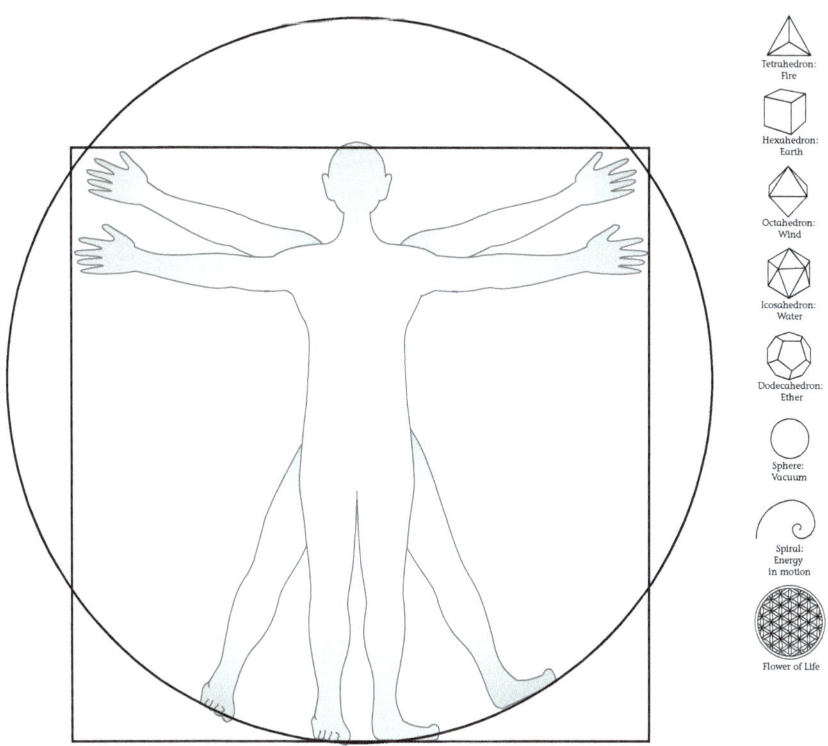

48- Anatomical proportion

This is Catsanasen's version of Leonardo da Vinci's famous drawing called the Vitruvian Man. This drawing gives origin to the Renaissance period and shows us the anatomical proportion of the human being.

Taking the navel as a central point and using a compass, the movements and positions of arms and legs would delimit a cube and a sphere leaving the Man inside. Through this image and making some inquiries I have been able to glimpse the hidden intention of this drawing, the sacred and perfect geometric code contained in the golden proportion in man and in

all of nature. These human proportions extend to the universe. The number of the golden ratio 1.6 is directly related to the sixteen positions that can be obtained from the combination of arms and legs. These movements speak of states of consciousness, in which man is evolving and reaching higher vibration, until he reaches the Christ consciousness. Later on you will see how Plato's solids are contained in the flower of life and how in this remembered drawing by Leonardo da Vinci he relates the anatomical proportion of the human being to the creation of the flower of life. Such solids are also called "perfect polyhedrons", because they all fit perfectly inside the cube. Solids are the geometrical codes that weave the flower of life, or rather, they are the codes that create life and give rise to man. Observe the image, let this information enter your mind, process it and meditate.

BODIES AND ITS DIMENSIONS

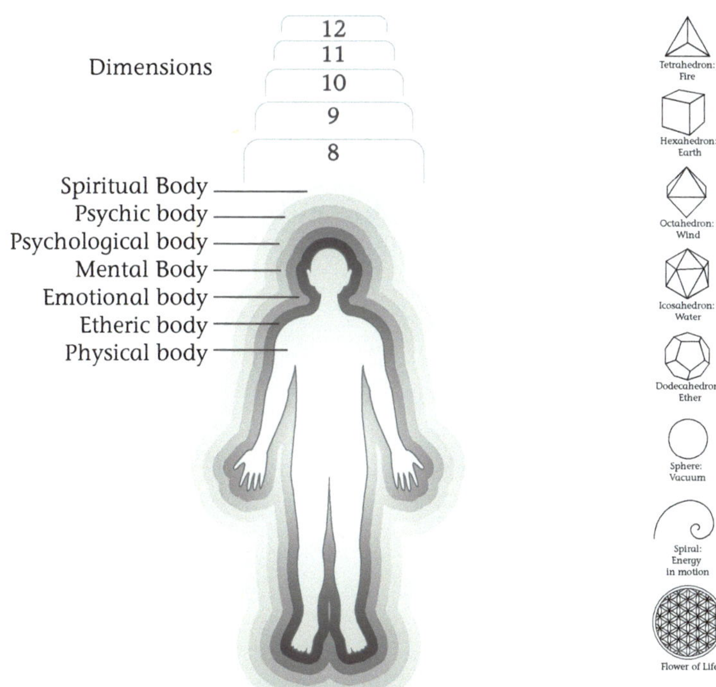

49- Bodies and its dimensions

In the image you are observing, the subtle bodies you already know are shown, and now, to enter into a more expanded consciousness over your entire energetic body, the dimensions are also schematized. It is not that they are really like that, like arches behind you, but they were given a shape for the brain to make a record of. In reality, the dimension is a state of consciousness.

As you see, five arcs have been drawn that end up giving a dimension up to the number 12 and you say why? because we have considered the following: the physical body as dimension number 1, the etheric body as dimension number 2, the emotional body as dimension number 3, the mental body

as dimension number 4, the psychological body as dimension number 5, the psychic body as dimension number 6, the spiritual body as dimension number 7, leading us to a stage of dimension number 8, stage of dimension number 9, stage of dimension number 10, stage of dimension number 11 and stage of dimension number 12. You will see later that these dimensions coincide with the number of spheres that the flower of life contains.

Simply observe and let this integrate into your brain to have a more expanded awareness of yourself without your limits.

THE NADIS
YOUR ENERGY BODY

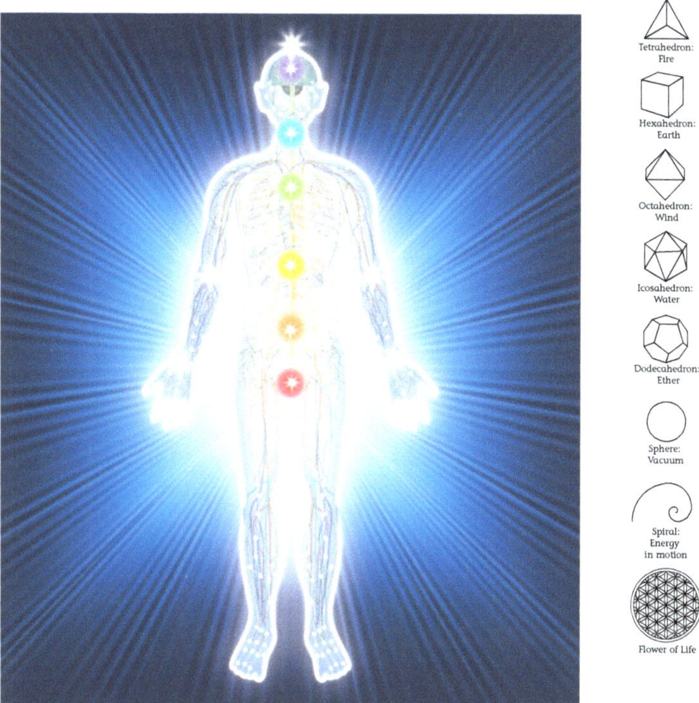

50- Nadis

Through the energetic body circulates all the energy that runs and gives life to your body. Through these conduits circulates the information of external energy and also the internal energy; they are etheric conduits through which passes the prana or vital energy. Observe this photograph and you will see that you can also see the bones, the nervous system, the circulatory system, the *chakras* and the expansion of the electromagnetic vibration of the aura, that is to say, that everything is connected.

As we explained in other photographs in the section "Deepening" through the energy that enters the *chakras*, passes through the nadis and is distributed through the rest of the

body reaching the blood. This is a different way of seeing the different subtle bodies and the different dimensions.

Observe the image calmly and try to identify the energy field that borders your physical body and detect if you find any conduit that is blocked or obstructed or the area. As we did with the meridians, choose a geometric figure and start applying it so that the communication between the different systems (energetic, circulatory, lymphatic and nervous system) is fluid, reaching your blood and your bones.

Therefore, try to identify where you can find what is blocked, and remember that the easiest way is to let intuition guide you by showing you where the blockage is; ask and the answer will come to you and simply give the order for the geometry to enter and do its work of atomic and molecular energetic reorganization in your body. Breathe, relax and work with tranquility.

MACRO POWER AND MICRO POWER CONNECTION

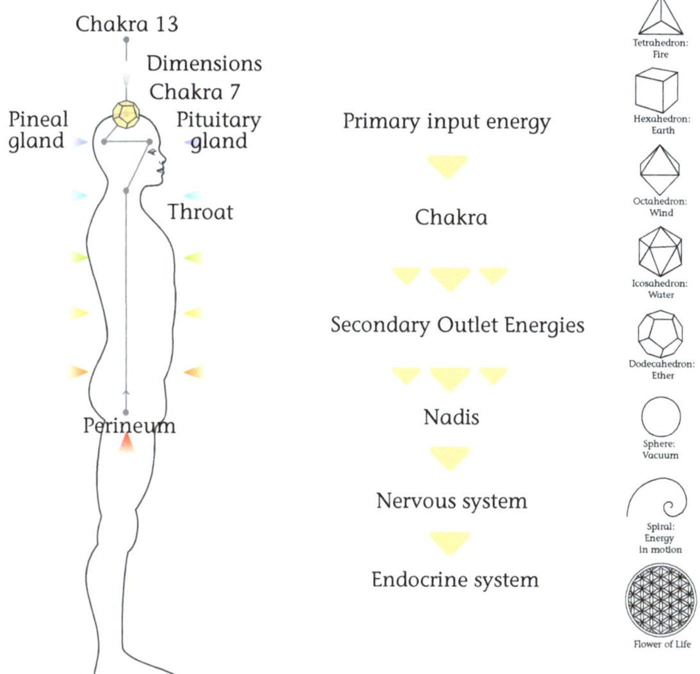

51- Macro and micro energy connection

This image tries to guide you visually in the route of the energy and its distribution in your body. Observe it and start from *chakra* number 13 (later you will know why we call it that) and go through all the dimensions you already know, from the 12th to the 7th *chakra*. Enter the seventh *chakra* and connect it with a dodecahedron, make this dodecahedron start working and connect your pineal gland and your pituitary gland with the energy you bring from the macro cosmos and take it to the *chakras*, so it will pass through: the sixth *chakra* which is at the level of the pineal and pituitary; the fifth *chakra* which is at the level of the throat; the fourth *chakra* in the chest; the third *chakra* in the solar plexus; the second *chakra* in the level of the

sacrum; and the first *chakra* in the perineum, and then continue visually with the energy down to the feet.

Once it has passed through all the *chakras* observe the scheme on your right, which says: "Primary energies of entry", and this is exactly what you have just done consciously; you have just made the energy enter through the *chakra*. Now become aware that this energy through the *chakra* begins to be distributed by the nadis (we saw them in the previous image), which are those etheric conduits through which the energy circulates. From the nadis it passes to your nervous system. Visualize your nervous system (if you do not remember, go back to "Deepening" and review it), from this system it passes to the endocrine system (where all the glands are), and from the latter this energy is distributed to the blood. So take your 10 minutes and make all these ducts be in perfect tune by visualizing how the energy enters and is distributed. If you notice that at any point there is a blockage use the geometry selection next to the image to unblock the area you have visually detected as being blocked. Take your time, register, go over the things you don't remember and practice.

ENERGY HEALING CHART

	LEVELS	PLATONIC SOLIDS
Karmas	Psychological Spiritual	
Curses	Emotional Psychological Spiritual Physica	
Traumas Past experiences Negative experiences	Mental Psychological Spiritual Physical	
Energy Inheritance	Emotional Psychological Physical Spiritual	
Phobias/Fears	Mental Emotional Psychological Physical	
Confusion Resistances	Mental Emotional Physical	
Guilt, sin and fear	Mental Emotional Physical Psychological Spiritual	

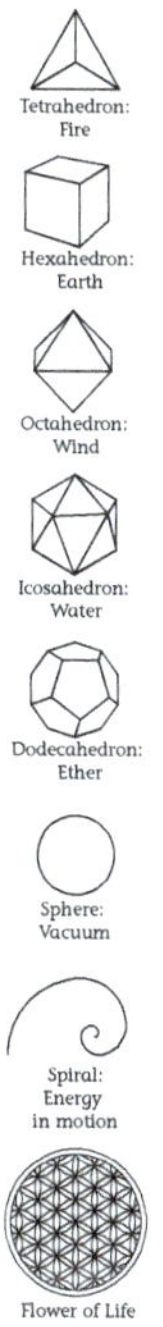

Tetrahedron: Fire
Hexahedron: Earth
Octahedron: Wind
Icosahedron: Water
Dodecahedron: Ether
Sphere: Vacuum
Spiral: Energy in motion
Flower of Life

52- Energetic Healing Chart

Here are presented what I usually call generators of distorted reality, which are karmas, curses, traumas, experiences lived in other lives, negative experiences, energetic inheritance, phobias, fears, confusions, resistances and a psychological and emotional triangle that generally works in the mind and which happens to be guilt, sin and fear. All these are generators of situations that are not real but that you live as if they were, that is why I call them distorted realities, because they provoke in you a distortion, generating the blockages that are presented in your life.

These are energetic vibrations, emotions or imprints that have remained in some way lodged in the physical body or in the different subtle bodies, so I recommend that if you do not remember your subtle bodies, you look again at the image of the physical body with the subtle bodies in order to have a general recognition again.

In the list in the first column to the left of the upper image you will see words like karma, curses, traumas, etc.; this list makes the choice much easier through intuition. So, I recommend that you intuitively go through the list with your eyes, from top to bottom and where your gaze stops and calls your attention (for example: energetic inheritance), observe what subtle bodies are involved, (in the case of energetic inheritance it would be: emotional, psychological, physical and spiritual). Very well, once you have identified it in your body, remember the drawing of the physical body with the subtle bodies, and what you should do next is to mentally apply the geometry presented next to the "Levels" column. There are many figures, I know, don't worry, what you can do is apply one moment and another moment, apply another. Remember that you work with intuition not with a structured mental scheme, so whatever way you choose will be the perfect shape. Allow yourself to play, allow the figure itself to come and do the work, let it choose the place; don't worry that it will work perfectly, allow it to happen, take your time, relax, do it quietly, select, apply the tool and meditate.

MAIN HEALING TETRAHEDRON
OF THE CATSANASEN METHOD VALID
FOR EVERY CIRCUMSTANCE

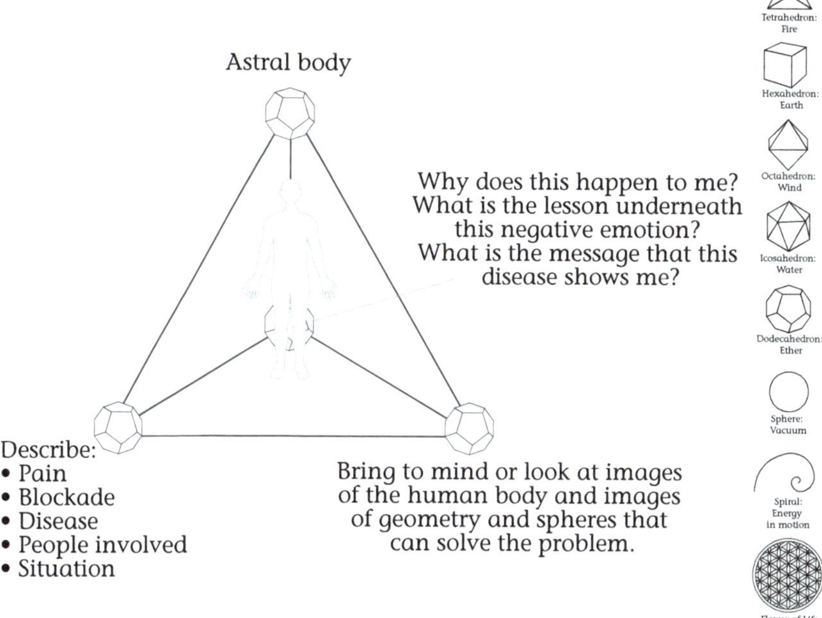

53- Main healing tetrahedron of the Catsanasen method valid for every circumstance

Every time you feel confused and do not know how to approach the work to heal some blockage or some situation you are living and need to solve, you have to do the following: sit comfortably and visualize a tetrahedron around you, in each corner a dodecahedron and place yourself as shown in the image. Do it visually or holographically, projecting the image you see here as if you were yourself or if you prefer you can also draw it, it works perfectly. Once you sit inside the tetrahedron you must place in one corner the blockage, the pain or the illness that you want to work on (as you see in the list on the left of this image) and in the other corner of your tetrahedron the geometric figures that according to your intuition will help you and in the case that the problem is physical you must add the part of the body that is involved (remember that

all this is mental and virtual work). You place yourself in the middle and in the other corner you place the questions: Why does this happen to me? What is the message that this illness is showing me, etc., (look at the list of questions in the image above or formulate a new one according to the occasion) and leave everything placed holographically in each corner as seen in the image. Place everything you want to work on and then connect mentally with the upper corner which would be the Astral Body. Let the tetrahedron begin to work together with the dodecahedra, take about 10 minutes, give the order to begin the work, relax, meditate and allow the healing to take place.

APPLICATION OF GEOMETRY FOR SPECIFIC POINTS

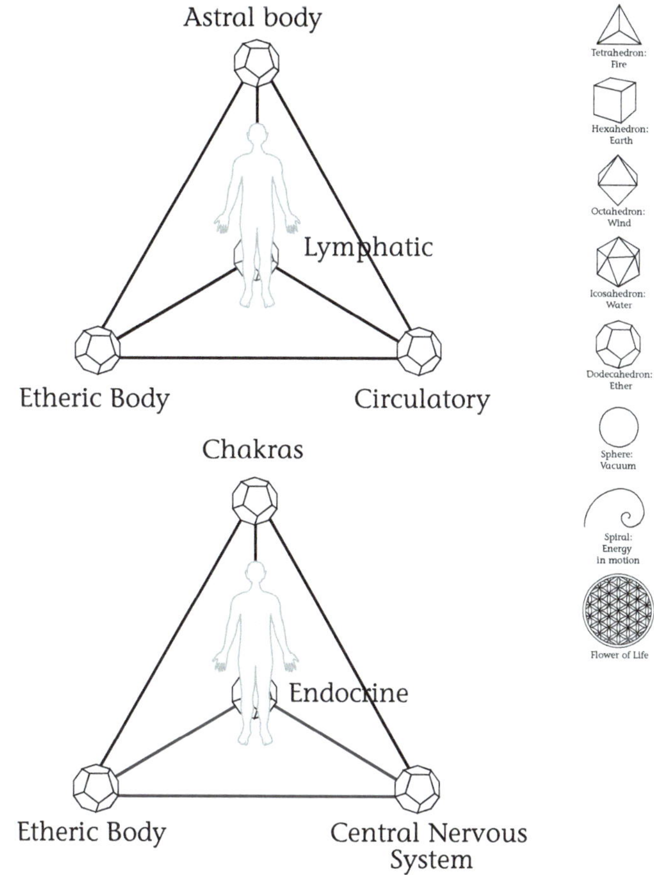

54- Application of geometry for Specific points

Focus and install a tetrahedron around you, visualize it and at each end you place a dodecahedron, as you have done in the previous image and as seen in this figure, but this time it will be to work on something specific, in this case the systems of your body.

Once the tetrahedron is installed, you connect to the etheric, circulatory, lymphatic and astral bodies. What you

are doing now is that, holographically and in different dimensions, you are reconnecting and cleaning in an energetic way the different bodies and the different points where you may find yourself blocked, a fact that interferes with the connection between the systems, bodies and its dimensions. You are presented with different tetrahedrons with different specific points to deal with, do one by one, take your time, practice them, and if you want or feel the need, you can place other points where these words are (such as the etheric body or central nervous system). Practice, first use the images that are here, do the cleansing, do the reconnection of these points and then apply other bodies or dimensions that you feel. For example: in this case there is not the psychological one, but you could add it, along with the etheric body, the endocrine body, the psychological body and the astral body or *chakras*. Make different combinations, but always remember to center and visualize your tetrahedron, the dodecahedra, and place the points you want to give the cleansing and reconnection. Practice, meditate, relax.

APPLICATION OF GEOMETRY FOR
SPECIFIC POINTS

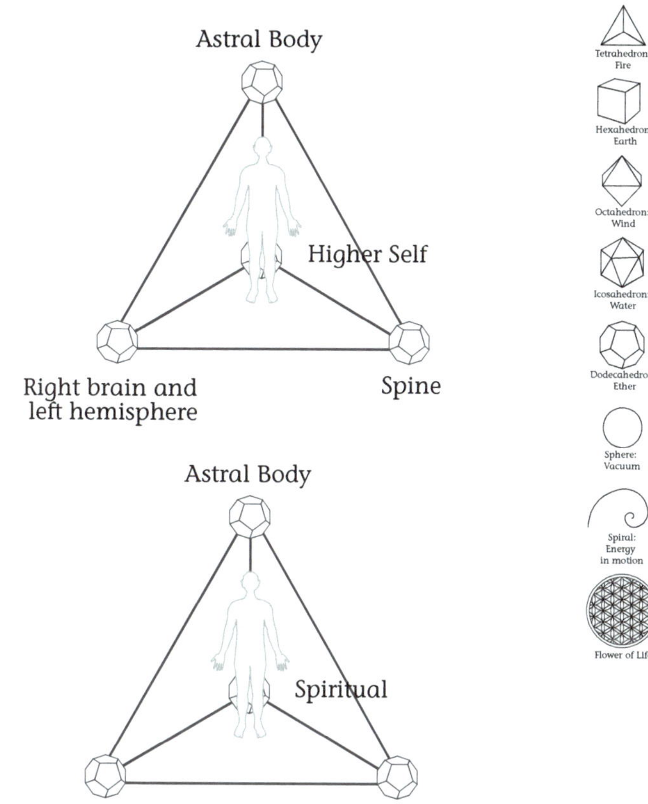

55- Application of geometry for Specific points

Here are some other combinations. As in the previous image, number 54, this one has the same indications; here we simply show you other combinations so that you can keep practicing and keep creating other possibilities. Work, create your own, detect where else you may have a blockage, and use this system which is very practical. Meditate, relax.

CONNECTION WITH VIBRATIONS, COLORS AND SACRED GEOMETRY

	LEVELS	SOLID
Hope	Reconnect emotional and physical body (heart and lungs).	
Sorry	Connection with the Forgiveness Vibration.	
Resentment	Emotional Mental Psychological	
Love	All levels and dimensions	
Third Eye	All levels and dimensions	
Divine Being	All levels and dimensions	
Awareness Energy	All levels and dimensions	
Male and female energy	All levels and dimensions	

Tetrahedron: Fire — Hexahedron: Earth — Octahedron: Wind — Icosahedron: Water — Dodecahedron: Ether — Sphere: Vacuum — Spiral: Energy in motion — Flower of Life

56- Connection with vibrations, colors and shapes

In this painting what I propose is that you go to the levels where certain vibrations are blocked, which is the way I have channeled it, and that you should apply the solids. For example: the vibration of hope often needs to be reconnected through the emotional and physical body, especially organs such as the heart and lungs. Well, in order to feel that vibration of hope again within you, I propose that you apply the colored

solids that you have in the column to the right of this picture as you see them, and if it seems very extensive or difficult to do, you can apply it one by one, or place them all together, or imagine yourself inside these solids, but it is necessary that you use the ones that are here drawn, in this order and with these colors; In this way what you do is to activate again the vibration of hope, of what hope means, of what hope is vibrating in you. You connect when you apply the solids, your emotional body with your physical body and you punctually focus on the heart and the lungs. As I have explained so far, the rest of the points to work on work more or less the same. In the forgiveness column you connect to the vibration of forgiveness by applying these solids; here there are no levels, it is your whole body and your whole being. When you do not see a specified level it means that you have to consider yourself with all the levels. Below the column of forgiveness, there is resentment, this is also a vibration and that vibration also acts and is activated on different levels. In this case I have detected that it is in the emotional, the mental and the psychological, although for you it could also be in another level; check it, and once detected you apply Plato's solids and, in this case, also Archimedes' solids, and simply let it act. Archimedes' solids have no color, if you want you can put a color, but in this case I propose them in, let's say, transparent. Let your mind simply draw the lines.

The vibration of love... yes, it carries all these solids! I know there are many, but don't worry, let the geometry work. You can see for example five dodecahedrons, but just putting a dodecahedron and imagine that the colors begin to change will be enough. When you see a geometrical figure repeat, let the figure come in and change color until the shape changes too, and then imagine that you come inside and move on to the next geometry. Dodecahedron, hexahedron, octahedron, icosahedron, sphere, octahedron and tetrahedron at the end. Go through all these shapes and all these colors and apply them on all your levels and in all dimensions to reconnect with the frequency of love.

The same to obtain the vibrational frequency that is activated by having the third eye activated; you do it on all levels

and in all dimensions. These codes that you see in the image are to apply these geometries and serve to activate your third eye. To connect with the energy of your divine being you have to do the same: connect with the shapes and colors that you see there. To have an energy consciousness you focus on yourself by entering with all your levels and dimensions into a dodecahedron, into a star and into the two solids of Archimedes. With the feminine and masculine energy you also do the same thing, and if you need it you go to the chapter of deepening where the Archimedes solids are, you visualize the images with their corresponding name and you then return to this image and apply it again.

Take your time, do it relaxed, it is not necessary to do all this scheme in one day, do one column at a time with its corresponding application. For example, the column of male and female energy one day of the week, the next day you work another column. Little by little feel and try, do it very slowly and centered. Meditate, practice, apply it.

CONNECTION WITH THE *CHAKRAS* OF THE HIGHER SELF

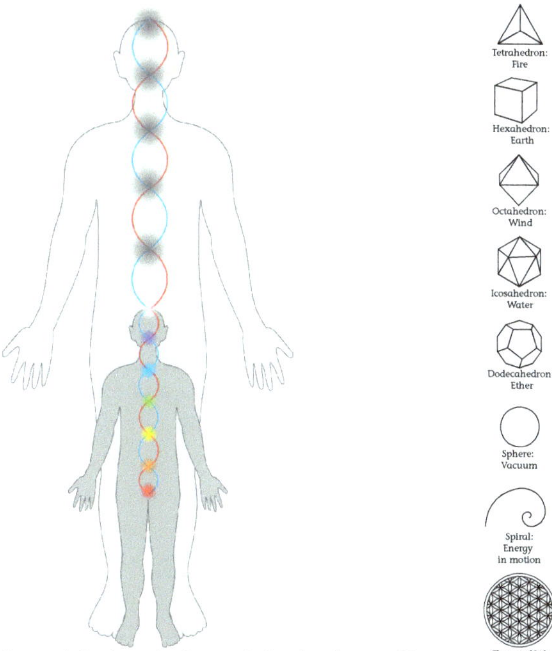

57- Connection with the *chakras* of the higher self

As you will see in this image there are two bodies: a much larger human figure than the one we have been seeing so far about the body and that we could also say that it is the older brother or superior being and a smaller human figure that would be the physical self, the personality. You will see that there are *chakras* in both the upper and lower figures. Until now you had seen the *chakras* of the physical self that connect your body and its dimensions to the physical self through *chakras* where the pranic energy passes through, but now there is a superior self or older brother with *chakras*, energy vortices and in this case there are five more extra corporeal *chakras*.

In previous images I had shown you the dimensions, we reached the twelfth dimension or the 12th dimension and we had outlined them with some simple arches. Now, what you

see with this image of an inferior self and a superior self with its *chakras* would be showing the total of *chakras* in the human being with its 12 dimensions. The superior self with five and the inferior self with seven, which gives a total of 12 dimensions or states of vibration.

To reconnect you are going to do the following: it is necessary that you sit down and relax, become aware of your first *chakra* and the following ones, begin to unite them with each other through these lines that are going up and creating energetic waves in the form of 8 with each central point of the *chakras*. You must consciously make the union of these lines; from the first with the second, and they continue and pass the lines from the second to the third, from the third to the fourth and they continue rising from the fourth to the fifth, from the fifth to the sixth and they reach the seventh. From your seventh *chakra* it passes to the first of your superior being or *chakra* number eight, whatever you want to name it. From the eighth *chakra* of your superior self pass to the ninth, continues to the tenth, which is at the level of the throat of your superior being, to activate the voice of the highest consciousness of you, from there passes to the eleventh which is at the level of the symbolic ears of the superior being and finally to the twelfth *chakra*, which is the last. Take your time, make your mind aware, unify them, visualize it as more comfortable for you and allow the energy lines you imagine to unite them. Meditate, relax, give intention and strength to the mind when joining the *chakras*.

APPLICATION OF COLOR ON SUBTLE BODIES

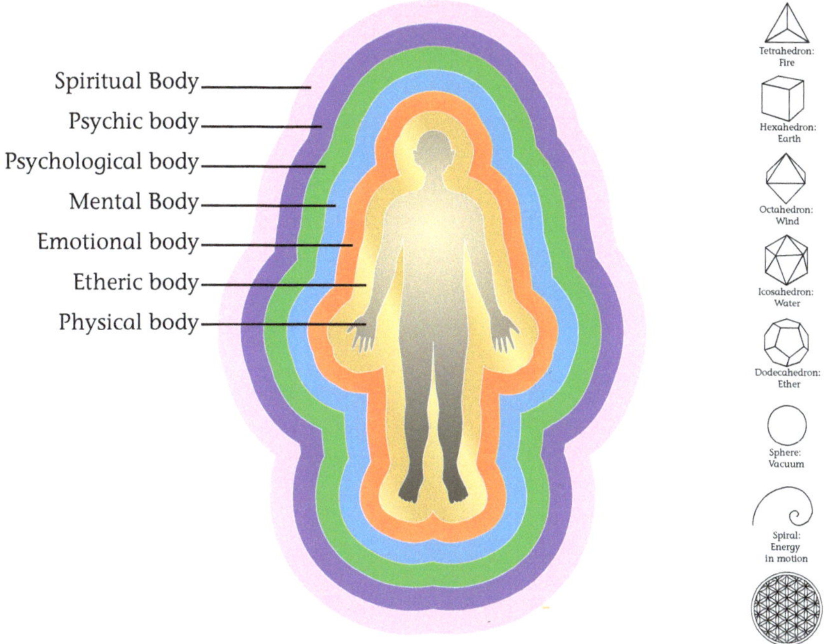

58- Application of color on subtle bodies

In this image we have placed colors in the subtle bodies you already know. You have to focus, relax and imagine the colors in your different subtle bodies. Remember that the dynamic of copy and paste works very well, as if you were dealing with a computer: give the command to your brain to copy and paste the colors into the subtle bodies. It's that easy. In the case of the physical body, as you see in this image, it has been given a neutral tone merely in order not to leave it white, but it is not necessary nor is it my intention that you apply a color in your physical body; it is only from the etheric body that you are going to apply the colors starting in the etheric body with gold, in the emotional body with orange, in the mental body with blue, in the psychological body with green, in the psychic body with violet and in the spiritual body with pink.

Once this application is made you will feel the cleansing in all your bodies because you will work with the vibration of these colors, which will generate a vibration in your subtle bodies and will make an energy healing and adjustment that will eliminate what does not correspond to each body in terms of energy and vibration. If you wish to make an application with other colors I recommend that you first do it as this image says, which is how I have channeled it, and then make another visualization or another meditation work with the application of the color that comes to you or that you feel would favor you in some subtle body or in all of them in general. Do it quietly, relaxed, use your intuition, work, apply, experience the feeling.

ETHER CONNECTION

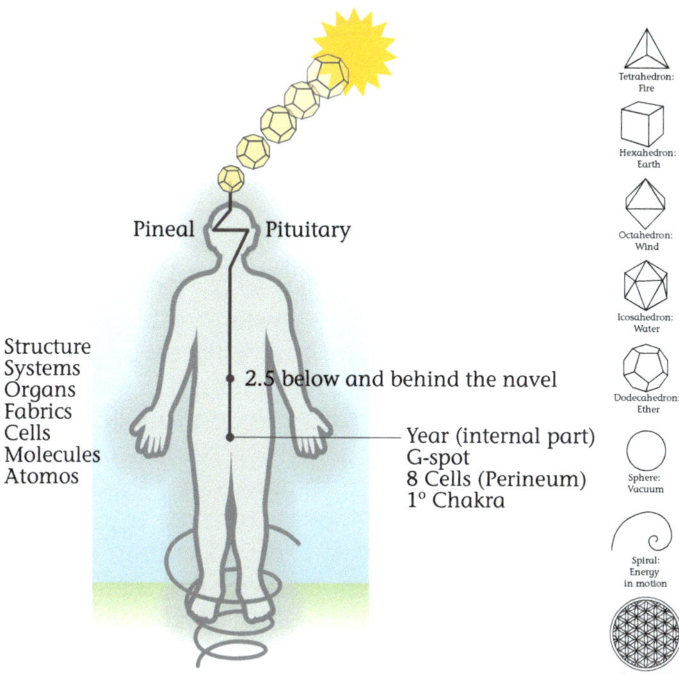

59- Conexión con el éter

As we have been studying, each solid is associated with an element: the dodecahedron is associated with the ether, the hexahedron with the earth, the icosahedron with water, the tetrahedron with fire, and the octahedron with air.

In this image I propose the idea that you visualize a dodecahedron that works with the element ether to connect you to the energy of the sun. Why? because the ether, in the past, was known as the lightest, or rather, extremely light substance that could unite all things, that filled all the spaces of things with each other. Let us say that somehow it united spirit to matter and what is in between is filled by the ether; it is what communicates spirit with matter, the lightest with the densest.

So to connect well with the particles of sunlight I propose that you do what I do, when I go for a walk or sit down to

meditate in the sunlight. I begin to visualize a dodecahedron that expands and connects with the particles of the sun. Those particles that we see when we look at the sun are attracted to me, they enter through my seventh *chakra* and connect the pineal and the pituitary. It is important to have these glands well placed in your head. That solar energy keeps going down in a straight line as you see it in the image until it reacheS 2.5 cm below and behind the navel, which is an energetic point or also called tantien. It is the central point or the energetic point from which all life, all the energy of your body, expands. From there you continue down to the point that is indicated in the image, the lower part between your legs, genital area, at this point, take the energy mentally aware of the inner anus in men or the G-spot in women, which is located inside the vagina. Between the anus and the genitals is the perineum, as I mentioned in "Deepening", which is the area of skin with more flesh and muscle between the anus and vagina in women and between the anus and the penis in men, and this connects with the first *chakra*, which you have identified enough for all the times we have seen the images with the *chakras*. Take your time and follow this whole journey, but first if you need, identify in your body the different parts as I said: the anus, G-spot, the perineum and the first *chakra*. Once you have identified this in the route (from the dodecahedron to the first *chakra*) you will see to the left of this image a text that names: structure, systems, organs, tissues, cells, molecules and atoms, that will help you with the intention to become conscious of taking the solar energy to your structures, systems, organs etc.

In this visualization we are connecting the solar light with important energetic points of our body. This work will revitalize these named areas and remove the memories of the traumas that are lodged there.

CONNECTION TO THE FIFTH CHAMBER
OF THE HEART

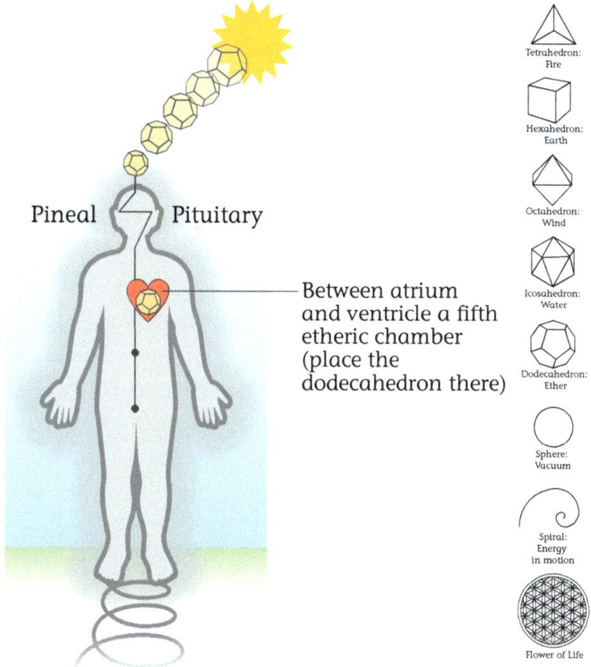

60- Connection to the fifth chamber of the heart

It is known that the heart is a muscle that contracts and expands, and we also know that this muscle fiber is as if rolled up on itself and inside this muscle are cavities called atria and ventricles. With this we are just naming the physical organ, but as we have been saying it is important to be aware of the etheric part of our whole body.

The etheric body is an exact energetic template of all that we have physically; in the case of the heart, its etheric part is presented as a fifth chamber and that is why it is called the fifth chamber of the heart. Sometimes, in this space, pain can remain engraved, stagnant and anchored, and it is important to be able to reach here in order to eliminate and dissolve it. I propose that you do the same meditation that we did with the previous figure: connect the ether through the dodecahedron

from the sun with its particles, descend the energy of the sun with the dodecahedron entering the seventh *chakra*, connecting the pineal with the pituitary, reaching your heart, entering the fifth chamber, and if you want you do a previous visualization, and try to find this space within your heart place the dodecahedron and allow it to start working. It is very possible that you have sensations, emotions that move, it is only energy that was stagnant, do not be afraid, do not worry, you will feel a movement until this that was anchored dissolves and leaves. Then you follow the midline of your body and reach your tantien (which is marked with the first black circle you see in the image) and finally you go down to the perineum, which you also know from the previous images.

Perform this meditation quietly, concentrate on cleaning the entire depth of the heart, its atria and ventricles and especially the fifth etheric chamber of the heart.

CONNECTION WITH PINEAL, PITUITARY AND HEART

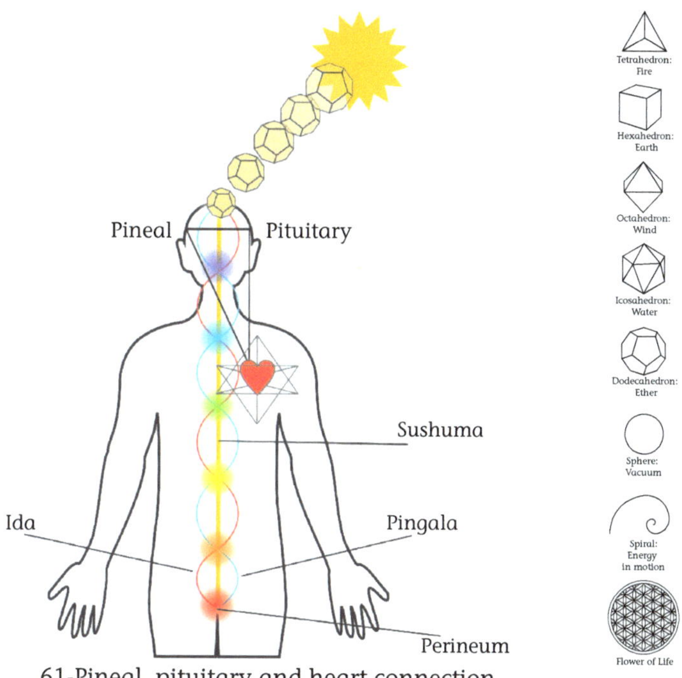

61-Pineal, pituitary and heart connection

The first thing I want you to observe in this image is the straight central line of the body (yellow) and at the sides of it, making the form of an eight, two lines that cross up and down connecting each of the *chakras*. We had seen it in a previous image and had spoken of the nadis as conduits through which pranic energy, vital energy, circulates. The main channels of the nadis are these 3 that are being shown to you here: the sushuma, ida and pingala, one on each side.

First you visualize them, you focus, you detect them in your body and you try to connect your *chakras* with these undulating energies, these conduits that are making this connection between the *chakras*, then we will proceed with the meditation. We began connecting with the dodecahedrons to the sun, we went down that central conduit and connected pineal with pituitary (remember where you have them located), continues down and cross the *chakras*, and from the pineal and pituitary, it's like moving an energy line that connects them with the heart. You know the *merkaba* star, we activated it in the " Beginning " level, so I want you to visualize your heart wrapped in the *merkaba* star and connect the pineal and pituitary gland to your heart star, once the connection is made, you keep going down intercrossing the *chakras* until you can reach the perineum. This connection requires more time, more attention, more concentration; do it in parts if you are not very sure and then try to visualize everything along with this whole system of energy conduits and try to synchronize and realize it as a whole. Take your time, relax and practice.

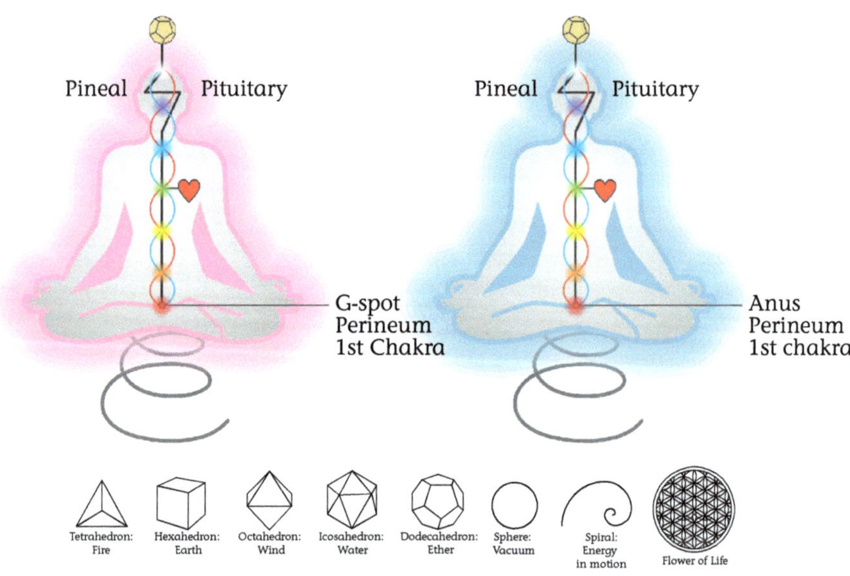

62- Connection with pineal pituitary and heart

We continue with the connection between the pineal, pituitary gland and the heart as in image 62, but here we will continue downwards and connect, in the case of the woman (figure delimited in pink), with the point G, the perineum and the first *chakra*, and in the case of the man (figure delimited in blue), with the anus, the perineum and the first *chakra*. Both the G spot in the woman and the anus in the man, in whose internal part there is a point similar to the G spot, these are very important energetic points; they are places where a lot of information is recorded, a lot of pain, the lived trauma, and many times it is here where the energy is blocked more. With these points unblocked we generate more vitality, more energy and better use of the vital and sexual energy we have, so it is important that you make the connection, if you want from the sun as in the previous figure or simply visualize a dodecahedron and do what we were doing: you go down the dodecahedron by your seventh *chakra*, you go to the pineal and pituitary gland, you start interlacing the *chakras* with the energy, you go to the heart, you keep going down and you focus, in the case of women, on the G-spot and in the case of men, on the inner point of the anus, then you go to the perineum and from there to the first *chakra* and you go down to the earth visualizing the energy in a spiral.

Meditate, relax, investigate and practice.

CONNECTION EARTH, BODY AND PLANETS

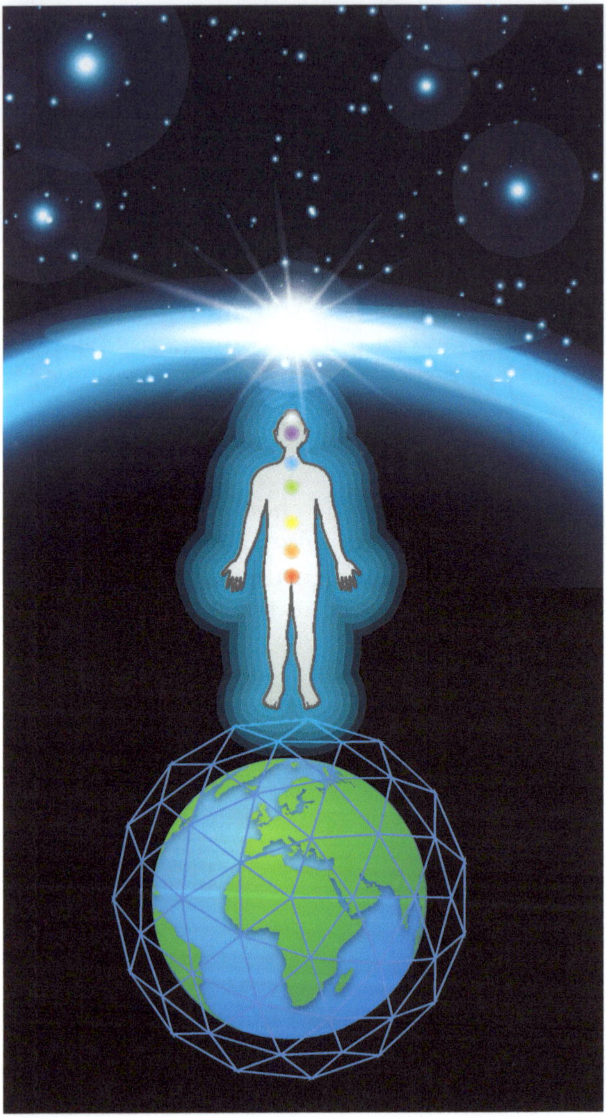

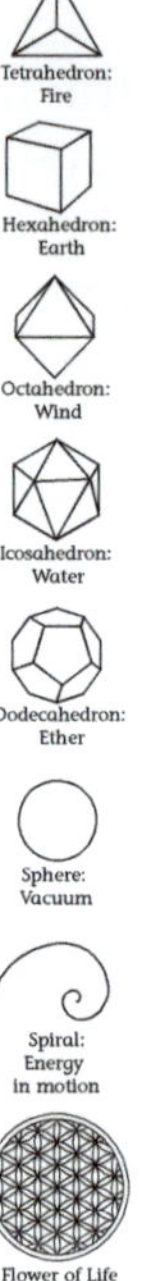

63- Connection earth, body and planets

While I was receiving the information that I channeled and wrote in this book, about how to apply sacred geometry, very clear images came to my mind, and showed me how the connection between earth, man and space is, and with these images that you see here represented I try to show you what I could see.

I propose you to observe the image, to become aware of your body, space and earth, as it is presented in the image (63) and as you can see the earth is presented with an icosahedral energy mesh that supports the planetary connection to which all human beings are energetically connected. We function as a kind of antenna, as a connecting cable between the earth and the cosmos.

Observe this image and imagine that you connect your feet on the ground and your seventh *chakra* to the cosmos allowing you to channel the information that you need to receive from the cosmos and from the earth. Take your time, visualize, channel this information and let it act on you.

THE *MERKABA* STAR

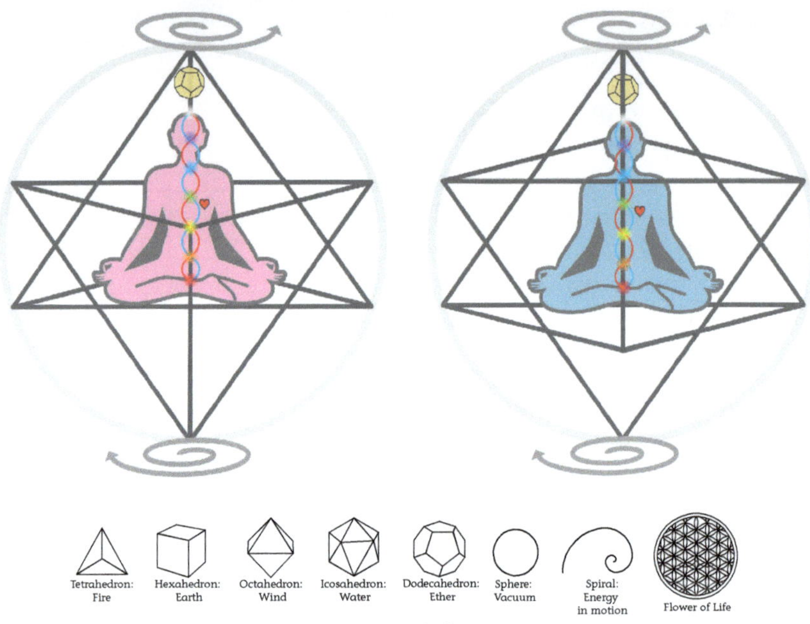

64- The *Merkaba* star

We have already met the *Merkaba* star on the " Beginning " level. Here we will add the dodecahedron and the connection with the energy channels Ida, Pingala and Sushuma, which are the three main channels of the nadis, and also with your heart. Reconnect with the dodecahedron this energy circuit that runs through your central line, your spine, and the connection to the heart. Reconnect with all of this, re-form the star tetrahedron as you did in " Beginning " and now try to activate all the dynamics of these energy connections with visualization to feel it more present and more firmly in your body. Practice, meditate.

CREATING REALITIES

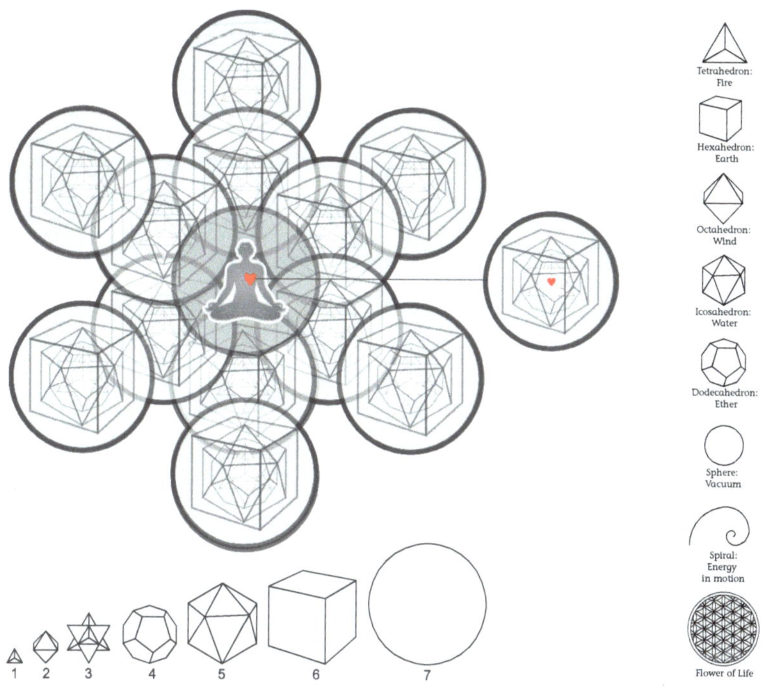

65- Creating realities

At the beginning of this level we saw in the stages of the flower of life the fruit of life, which is a stage where you see thirteen spheres; this is the leap from the 12th dimension to the 13th dimension.

What you see in the center of the circles is you meditating within your sphere and creating the fruit of life. Your thirteen spheres are created by the movements of the geometries below you: the tetrahedron, the octahedron, the star *merkaba*, the dodecahedron, the icosahedron and the hexahedron, they are all contained in sphere number 7 of the line of geometric figures (the one you see below the general picture).

These thirteen spheres are the thirteen dimensions that we have also seen before with the subtle bodies and that we have

represented with arcs; now we are creating thirteen realities that are going to begin to be created around you, inside each sphere you must place the intention of what you want to see accomplished in your life. But in order for these realities to be well balanced it is important to clean them and reorganize them energy wise, placing the solids in the order we have given them you will be able to balance and organize this energy.

As you will see in the human figure sitting in the center, a sphere with geometries comes out of its heart, it is simply a visual amplification of what you have to do in your heart; you must also surround your heart with this sphere and the indicated geometries so that the energy is also rearranged in the heart. What you have to do exactly is to visualize your heart within these geometries, make one sphere at a time until later you can do it with your mind in all spaces and dimensions. Practice, relax, meditate.

THE FLOWER OF LIFE

66- The flower of life

As you may remember, we started this journey of self-healing at the " Beginning " level and the first image we saw was the flower of life. In "Liberation" we ended up with the flower of life, but here it comes accompanied by the image of the man from Vitruvius (Catsanasen version), which shows the anatomical proportion within a sphere and a square, which makes more sense when we now superimpose the flower of life on it, because of all that we have been learning and that we know that geometry creates life.

What you see here is telling you that through sacred geometry we can reconstruct, reorganize and balance our subtle,

and multidimensional physical body. I don't know if Leonardo knew this or not, but somehow he whispered to us that inside the sphere and inside the cube there was a perfect human who could raise his consciousness. What was not said then, is that Platonic solids are geometric codes and that through visualization and application in the physical and subtle body we can reorganize and balance atoms and molecules, which may be distorted or blocked, so we can reorganize a cell, reconstruct a tissue, dissolve a tumor, etc. The intention with which we impregnate the image in order to heal directly is what will make the quantum leap towards the change you desire.

Connected to intuition and directing the energy of the forms that we visualize, we can change all that we want. This is what the latest photograph of the flower of life and the drawing of Leonardo da Vinci is showing you, and my intention is that thanks to this Catsanasen methodology, you become aware that you are the creator and remodeler of your body. I suggest you to practice this last meditation: visualize yourself inside a cube where you can fit all the platonic solids, try to imagine them inside, this will give you the Metatron's Cube. Once you have achieved this image, you add the sphere and on top of it the flower of life. That is: you inside the cube that contains all the solids inside the sphere creating the flower of life.

Remember that your body is made up of atoms and molecules, which are composed of energy, and you can modify the energy with the intention of your thought; so go deep within yourself and modify everything that you desire and produce the internal and external change that you expect in order to have a better life.

Thank you.